Feng Shui

Demystified

By Clear Englebert

THE CROSSING PRESS
FREEDOM, CALIFORNIA

For information on bulk purchases or group discounts for this and other Crossing Press titles, please contact our Special Sales Manager at 800/777-1048.

www.crossingpress.com

Library of Congress Cataloging-in-Publication Data

Englebert, Clear.
    Feng shui demystified / by Clear Englebert.
        p. cm.
    ISBN 1-58091-078-5 (pbk.)
    1.Feng-shui I. Title.

BF1779.F4 E54 2000
133.3'337--dc21   00-030713

Acknowledgments

I offer gratitude to Steve Mann, Rick Mears, Susan Levitt, Caryle Hirshberg, and Elaine Gill. Their help and encouragement was instrumental in the birthing of this book. I also offer eternal thanks to my wonderful parents, Merle Twitty Englebert and Robert William Englebert. They were public school teachers for a combined sixty-two years. My teaching ability is largely inherited from them. I most humbly thank the woman who ordained me a Zen Buddhist, Reverend Master Jiyu-Kennett (Order of Buddhist Contemplatives).

Table of Contents

Preface   9

Introduction   11

CHAPTER 1   The Exterior   13
                 Approach   13
                 Front Door   18
                 Foreboding Objects   20
                 Lay of the Land   23

CHAPTER 2   Chi Flow   27
                 Loss of Chi   30
                 Clutter   35
                 Empowered Positions   40
                 Other Positions   45
                 Poison Arrows   47
                 Attracting Chi   52

CHAPTER 3   Introduction to the Bagua   57
                 Chart of Bagua Areas   60
                 Elemental Cycles   62

CHAPTER 4   The Bagua in Place   65
                 Applying the Bagua   70
                 Individual Bagua Areas   72
                 Bathroom Location   83
                 Fireplaces   87

CHAPTER 5   Extensions and Missing Areas   89
                 Bringing Back a Missing Area   91
                 Window Boxes   93

CHAPTER 6   Architectural Features   97
                  Doors   97
                  Windows   99
                  Poles   101
                  Kitchens   102
                  Home Offices   105
                  Bedrooms   107
                  Highrise Apartments   110
                  Air Circulation   111

CHAPTER 7   Furniture and Household Objects   113
                  Beds   113
                  Glass Tabletops   115
                  Altars   116
                  Clocks   119
                  Mirrors   120
                  Symbolism   122
                  Living Room Furnishings   124

CHAPTER 8   Other Considerations   125
                  Yin/Yang   125
                  Moving   128
                  Locating a New Home   129
                  Repairs and Renovations   131
                  Guests   133
                  Pregnancy   136
                  The Number Four   137
                  Organizing   138
                  Vibrational Cleansing   140
                  Used Objects   144
                  Non-Feng Shui Techniques   145

CHAPTER 9	Gardening	147
	Landscaping	147
	Pruning	150
	The Five Elements	152
	Houseplants	154
	Thorny Plants	155
CHAPTER 10	Retail Stores	157
	The Front	158
	Physical Layout	160
	Business Hours	162
CHAPTER 11	Offices	163
	Waiting Rooms	165
CHAPTER 12	Vehicles	167
	Cars	169
	Trucks, Vans, and RVs	170
Appendix I	Recommended Books	171
	Compass Orientation	172
	Entrance Orientation	174
	Related Topics	177
Appendix II	Glossary	181
Appendix III	Chinese Astrological Signs and Elements	187

Preface

This book may introduce some words and concepts that are new to you. I have put these in the glossary in the back of the book which will direct you to the page where the term is dealt with in depth.

Introduction

It is pronounced *fung shway* and it means wind/water. It is the part of ancient Chinese Taoism that is concerned with how objects affect energy and how that energy affects your life. It has survived four millennia because it actually works. The efficacy of feng shui isn't something you have to take on faith. If done correctly, it can prove itself for anyone. Some aspects of feng shui seem like common sense, while others seem like total superstition. There are about as many different kinds of feng shui as there are kinds of Christianity.

Even though feng shui came from the East and partakes of those philosophies, it is very much concerned with universal energetics. It is wise to educate yourself as to how energy flows and to know how the things around you are influencing you. The way certain chairs are positioned can make a big difference in how prepared you are for the future. The shape of the landscape around your home *is* influencing you. The location of knives and the shape of windows can say something about how people get along with one another in a particular house.

Some aspects of Western interior design and architecture are anathema to feng shui. The following are quite common, and are considered to be serious problems:

- Walls of glass (which let chi leak out fast)

- Glass tabletops (acting like blades, cutting you off from reaching your goals)

- Open beams (which radiate poison arrows to the space below them)

Some items associated with feng shui clash with sleek modern design. Windchimes (where there is no wind), hanging flutes, big fake firecrackers, statues of Taoist deities, Chinese coins on a string, bagua mirrors, and prismatic crystals are viewed by some as Chinese knickknacks. Others see them as welcome, if eclectic, additions to their home. My firm belief is that there is always a way to express the *intention* of a feng shui solution in any décor.

Yes, you *can* do it yourself! There are precious few situations so onerous that only a professional feng shui consultant can solve them. You must be willing to experiment, study like a fiend, and continually view your place with unemotional eyes. If you, the resident, are willing to put your emotions about objects and their arrangement aside, even briefly, you will surely be more effective in your feng shui applications. Finally, and I do believe most importantly, is intuition. Listen to it, cultivate it, act on it.

CHAPTER 1

The Exterior

APPROACH

The physical environment around a dwelling can have a great impact upon the residents. The outside is where energy (chi) finds you first. Put yourself in the position of a first-time visitor.

- Your *house (or apartment) number* should be very clearly visible. If it is appropriate, also have your name visible on the outside. An address number will benefit from having each digit placed slightly higher than the digit to its left.

- *Brilliant red* attracts chi energy more than any other color. Red objects (such as red flowering plants or plants in red glazed pots) near the street on each side of your driveway or walkway act as a stop sign to chi. "Stop, chi energy! Come in here!" Maximize the effect by repeating it near your front door. Realistic artificial plants can be used, but must be replaced when they fade. Faded artificial plants do not attract chi energy and, in a sense, they repel it.

- *A large object, such as a tree or bush, that is in a direct line between the street and your front door* bodes ill. I'm a great lover of trees, but this is not the right place for one. Think of it this way: the chi energy is trying to come into your front door and is somewhat irritated by having to veer around the tree—and that's the main energy coming into your life! If the obstruction is not removable, it is best to place a small bagua mirror above your front door. This kind of mirror has an eight-sided frame with different *I Ching* trigrams on each side. There is always a little hanging device on one side. Pay attention to that and keep that side up. It is considered to be powerful and is primarily for exterior use. Bagua mirrors are usually quite inexpensive and are available in any major Chinatown. Most, however, are cheaply made and can start to look faded and tacky after a time. That, in addition to the fact that they look a bit too hocus-pocus for some tastes, may cause you to choose an alternative. Any mirror or very shiny reflective object (such as a brass door-knocker) will do. It is important that you feel comfortable with feng shui "cures" that you use. It is, after all, *your* home!

- If the *pathway leading to your front door* from the street or sidewalk is a very direct line, it needs to be tempered a bit. It's best if the chi meanders up to your front door instead of charging right in. One way to do this is by placing flowerpots (or other interesting outside ornaments) on the sides of the steps or pathway. By having the pots in a staggered pattern (not directly across from each other as in a formal arrangement) the visual energy is forced to zigzag and therefore slow down. If the pots are themselves interesting or whimsical and each one is different, the solution will be even more effective.

- If the headlights of cars driving by shine onto your house on a regular basis, for example, if your house is in *a cul-de-sac or T-intersection*, it's time to plant a big fat hedge or put up a solid fence. If this isn't immediately feasible, then place a bagua mirror outside your house facing the headlights. A convex mirror is an excellent alternative to a bagua mirror in this circumstance. You are basically saying "no" to that energy and sending it back.

- It is best if *the garage* is not more prominent than the front door. If the garage is most prominent, it sends the energetic message that at least one of the people who lives there will be away from home a lot. About the only thing you can do in this case is to work to make your front door area more noticeable. You can formalize it with matching planters on each side of the door, distinctive lighting, bright paint, windchimes, or

whatever makes it stand out without looking out-
landish.

- If there are *stairs* going up to your front door, they
  need to have risers as well as treads. This is true for
  interior stairs as well, and I cannot overstress the
  importance of this. Risers are the vertical parts of
  stairs that connect the treads. When you walk upstairs
  the risers are the part that your toes are pointing
  towards. They are rarely a structural necessity but
  energetically they are vital. If you can see right
  through the stairs, the chi energy is doing exactly
  what your eyes are doing. It is slipping through the
  open spaces and moving on. It is not rising up to your
  living space where it needs to go.

  One woman could not add risers because she was a
  renter. Instead she stapled beautiful red oilcloth where
  the risers would have been. It was stunning and quickly effective.

  There are certain kinds of cement stairs that resist
  any kind of riser addition. This is one of the very few
  instances where feng shui says, "You might want to
  move!" You are missing a huge percentage of the chi
  energy that would otherwise be coming to you in your
  daily life. Moving is often not an option and if that's
  the case, do everything in your power to bring the
  visual energy continuously up the stairs. Matching red
  pots with matching plants on each side of each stair or

a vine (live or artificial) trailing up along the banister railing are two possible solutions. An exterior fountain or windchime near the door would be good. Also do everything you can to visually emphasize your front door. You probably can't overdo it because the situation is somewhat dire and calls for a "say something" front door.

FRONT DOOR

The front door is referred to as "the mouth of chi." The door that the architect intended to be the main entrance (where guests are usually received) is considered to be the front door for feng shui purposes. It doesn't matter whether or not another (side) door is used more frequently. If the front door has been completely blocked or nailed shut, then the secondary door becomes the new mouth of chi. In this instance, there are likely to be confused energies in the house. It would be best to go ahead and do whatever major remodeling it takes to totally erase the old front door and visually establish the new one. Other things to consider about the front door are:

- It should be the largest outside door—larger than any back or side doors.

- If there is also a screen (or storm) door, the hinges should be on the same side of the door frame as the main door. This applies to any outside door.

- The hinges should not squeak and the door should open and close easily without catching or scraping on anything. This applies to any and every door.

- Front doors should open *inward*, inviting the chi energy inside. If they open outward, it can be seen as repelling the chi. Don't worry if a screen door opens outward, they usually have to.

One of the fundamental aspects of a front door is that when it is closed, you should be able to have privacy. This also allows you to temper the chi flow. If the majority of the front door is clear glass, or if the areas immediately beside the front door are clear glass, chi can come and go any time, all the time—and it will! If someone standing outside your front door can see a lot of what is directly inside the door, you need some sheer curtains, either on the door or on the side windows next to it. On side windows, you may also use tall plants to provide privacy. Either option will still allow plenty of light to enter, which was undoubtedly the architect's intention.

If you're bold enough to paint your front door red, you're doing yourself a gigantic favor. If you can't bring yourself to paint it brilliant red, use whatever shade of red appeals to you.

FOREBODING OBJECTS

Threatening objects or poison arrows that aim at or loom toward your dwelling should be repelled with mirrors. Bagua mirrors are great, but any mirror will do. The use of outside (repelling) mirrors is both symbolic and quite real. It is best if the mirror is aimed exactly at the offending object. Some examples of threatening objects are:

- Large industrial smokestacks

- Large broadcasting towers

- Electrical transformers (fairly common)

- A building with a turret with a sharp cone top

- A cliff with large rocks that is close to and above your home

- A next-door neighbor's roof that is level with your window, with an excessive number of chimneys and vent fans

- Oversize church steeples

- A building with a large right angle pointed directly at your home. See Illustration #1, and Poison Arrows page 21.

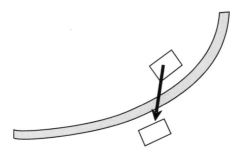

Poison Arrow from Another House

Illustration 1

If the object that you're repelling is quite large, a concave mirror will symbolically shrink it as well as repel it. A convex mirror is often best to repel the energy of a very busy road, like a freeway.

In addition to the outside mirror, you might consider putting these things inside the window:

- A large plant rising up from below the window

- Crystal/windchimes/mobile in that window

- Sheer or lacy curtains in the window

- A shoji screen

- Heavy drapes

Churches, especially those that are visually prominent with large steeples and crosses, are not considered to be good chi neighbors. Their exaggerated size, when viewed strictly as an environmental landform, is often foreboding. Also, funerals are conducted there and many religious traditions believe that a person's spirit can remain in close proximity to their body for several weeks after death. If you have a door opening directly toward a church or cemetery next door, put a mirror (bagua or other) over the outside of that door.

If you live right next to a cemetery, keep a small light on at all times in front of an image that you think of as sacred.

LAY OF THE LAND

The most ancient type of feng shui is the landform school, predating even the compass school. The energy of the lay of the land surrounding your dwelling can have a significant impact upon your life. The energy outside your home is represented by four animals:

- Green Dragon (masculine) on the left, if you are outside facing the front door

- White Tiger (feminine) on the right, if you are outside facing the front door

- Black Tortoise behind the house

- Red Phoenix in front of the house

The animals are considered archetypal and powerful. The shape and size of land features or other structures near your home is the energetic expression of these animals. The dragon and the tiger have potentially destructive energy. In the ideal situation they keep each other in check by being balanced. Therefore, large buildings or land features on either side of your home should seem balanced (when considering your house in the middle). If a large upward object on one side of your house is not balanced on the other side, then it's your job to bring about symbolic visual balance. "Symbolic" is the key word, because it is rarely feasible to create actual physical balance. A common solution is an exterior light pole in the side yard that needs the addition.

Light is one of the most powerful expressions of chi energy and can work wonders!

The tortoise and phoenix are in proper energetic alignment when the land in front of your house slopes down and the land behind your house slopes up. When you are standing inside your front door, looking out, the land should slope gently down toward the street or sidewalk. Behind your house the land should rise gently. That's the ideal. Now let's deal with the actual. Many houses do not have that landscape dynamic and something should be done to symbolically change the situation. If the land drops off dramatically behind your house, as is the case in many homes with "a great view," put a moving weather vane on top of your house to lift the energy upward. If you can add exterior lighting, do so with uplights, which shine upward onto the building. Also, if it is possible, add a fountain outside your front door with the water flowing away from your front door. This solution is subtle, but powerful. If the fountain flows constantly, it will continually oppose the dynamic set up by the lay of the land. In fact, it is *always* a good idea to have a water feature (a small pond or gentle fountain) in your front yard. It reinforces the feeling that the front yard is lower than the back yard, because water flows down and "collects" in your front yard.

There is another aspect of landform, which involves the five elements. Your home, by its shape and construction materials, predominately represents one of the five elements. The area around your home is also determined to represent one of the five elements. The interaction between the two elements is then evaluated. For instance, an asymmetrical home with lots of glass is Water. When that home sits amid round mountains, it is in a Metal environment and that's good because Metal generates Water (see Elemental Cycles, page 62). The outside environment produces the same element of which the home is made, thereby feeding its prosperity. This concept is tricky and complicated and one of the most understandable explanations is in Damian Sharp's *Simple Feng Shui* (see Recommended Books). This knowledge is quite important for homeowners and those looking to buy a home.

CHAPTER 2

Chi Flow

Chi is just the Chinese name for what is perhaps the most basic thing in the universe—energy. Do not think of it as some ghostly, amorphous thing. You are a high expression of chi energy. When something gets your attention, chi energy is being drawn there. Your clue is the fact that you noticed it. Your neck muscles moved so that you could turn your head. Your eye muscles moved so that you could look toward that "something." Energy was required for those muscles to move. Madison Avenue is expert at attracting chi energy, even though the advertisers probably don't think of it that way. Light, movement, and sound are primary attractors of chi. That is why prismatic crystals and water fountains are recommended so often in feng shui.

It is not difficult to determine how chi flows within a building. If there are places where you are able to move quickly, such as a long straight hallway, chi energy is speeding right along. When this happens, the chi is packing a punch and is not considered to be very healthy. If there are places where your movement is very encumbered (such as corners that are overly filled with furniture, etc.), most likely chi energy is stagnating there.

Long straight hallways conduct chi too quickly. If the hall is wide enough, put one or more narrow tables along the walls. If multiple tables are used, stagger them on opposite sides. This causes the chi to zigzag and thereby slow down. If the hall is too narrow for tables, use pictures, mirrors, or wall sculptures. If it is possible to add lighting, do so with splashes of light playing on the walls. Make the hall so interesting and pleasant that one is tempted to linger there, as in an art gallery. Feel free to hang mobiles, windchimes, or crystals from the ceiling. Also if doors are left open or ajar along the hallway, this will cause chi to flow into those rooms rather than just zooming down the long hall. Keep doors to bathrooms and closets closed, however.

Do not let anything accumulate behind a door in such a way that the door cannot open to its fullest. The door is what allows the energy to enter the room. To whatever degree it is blocked, that amount of potential is not reaching your life. When a door opens, chi can flow in smoothly or it can sometimes get disturbed. A wall that confronts you as soon as you've stepped into a space is jarring to chi. It will help greatly to put a picture or mirror on that wall. The picture should have visual depth, such as a landscape. If the wall that confronts you has a door that is almost, but not quite, directly in front of you, the effect is disturbing in a slightly different way. It would be best to hang a crystal in the hall between the two doors. See Prismatic Crystals on page 53 for instructions on hanging crystals.

Drapes that puddle on the floor—drapes that are very long—affect chi in a good way. If the "pile of fabric" on the floor looks good (not dusty and dirty), it catches the eye, and the strong vertical line of the drape pulls the eye (and the chi) up. It is very healthy to cause chi to rise up like that, and even regular floor-length drapes will work fine.

LOSS OF CHI

Notice how your eyes move when you step inside a room and look around it. If there are things that get your attention, that's where chi is going first. A very common problem is a window or glass door directly opposite the entrance door. It is almost impossible not to look outside. That is exactly what chi does. It makes a beeline out of your place and it's gone! It can be miles away in an instant and it ain't coming back! Modern design often says let the view be most important. Feng shui says that if the view rules, the chi (attentive energy) of most people is going out of your home—to the view. This lets you know that chi energy in general is vanishing out that window. People may bemoan the loss of a great view, but it is often best to be close to a window before the fullest view is appreciated—on a porch or deck is preferred.

The most effective solution to this problem is to create "a showstopper" within your space. Place something that competes with the view in front of, or very close to, the view window or door. It can be as simple as a stunning orchid in bloom (for a small window) or (for a large expanse of glass) it may need to be something like a sculpture that grabs your attention and won't let go. However long your attention is held inside your space is valuable time. It gives chi time to flow around the room and fill up the corners. Remember that the color red acts as a stop sign to chi energy like no other color can. The effect you want to create is, "What a lovely orchid! Oh, and what a great view!" Let the view be a fabulous bonus that is discovered *after* the attention has stayed inside for a moment. Sometimes a moment is all you can hope for, but that's enough, as long as the dynamic that is created is *first* inside, *then* outside. Other suggestions to help hold chi in the room are:

- A *crystal or windchimes* hung in a direct line between the entrance and the view.

- Put *a bagua mirror* over the view window or door. This is one of about three times when it's okay (and advisable) to put a bagua mirror inside a house. Any time that I recommend a bagua mirror, please realize that *any* mirror will work.

- A *window box* can be perfect in certain situations. It stops the visual energy right outside the room and draws it back from a very distant and commanding view. See Window Boxes, page 93.

Overly large windows (i.e., walls of glass) and windowpanes which exactly meet in a corner allow chi energy to slide right out of your life. They also do not allow you any control of the chi pouring into your life. Consider using sheer drapes or stained glass panels, both of which go well with modern décor.

You've probably gotten the idea by now that chi behaves somewhat like moving water or wind. This is why drains are considered to be a problem. Chi wanders into your bathroom, finds several convenient drains, and flows right out of your house. Don't let it happen! Cover your drains to whatever degree is feasible. If a drain cannot have a stopper over it, then a hair-catching strainer is the next best thing. It at least reduces the visible size of the drain. Make sure the shower curtains or doors are closed in such a way that the drain is not visible. It is important to avoid mildew, so they can be left somewhat open for air circulation, if necessary. Just be sure that the drain itself isn't visible unless you poke your head into the shower area. The toilet lid must stay down at all times when the toilet is not in use. A lot of people seem to resist this rule. All I can say is, "Get over it and get used to it!" It is so important; it is a number one rule! It is also best to keep the bathroom doors closed, or only slightly ajar (if air circulation is an issue). Mirrors on the outside of bathroom doors are almost always a good idea. They work in two ways: by reflecting and repelling the chi and keeping it from going into the bathroom in the first place, and by sealing off the body waste energy of the bathroom from the rest of the house. The silvering on the back of the mirror has a symbolic sealing effect. If a bathroom opens directly into a kitchen, it is *vital* that the door stay closed and be mirrored. Foods to eat and body waste to expel are opposite energies and their vibrations need to be quite separate. Within a kitchen, all drains should be closed or at least have strainers.

If there are sticks in your house (any kind of sticks: lumber, walking sticks, driftwood, or dried stick arrangements) that are somewhat vertical and are touching the floor (or in a floor vase), remove them. When chi encounters those sticks it is conducted down and out. It is especially bad when the sticks are in the Fortunate Blessings area.

If stairs to the upper floor are directly in front of (and facing) the entrance door, the chi may not stay inside your house. Imagine the chi bounding into your home, heading directly up the stairs, then just rolling right back out your front door. That's pretty much what happens. It probably does not happen if the stairs are more than approximately twelve feet from the door. In that case the chi has plenty of time to "get curious" about the lower floor and begin to circulate there. Stairs that are closer than twelve feet to (and directly facing) the front door would benefit from having a large potted plant at the bottom. The plant form should be uprising, not drooping. An umbrella stand can also work, symbolically catching the chi that is trying to leave. Putting a bagua mirror inside, above the door, is also recommended. This is another instance when it is okay to put a bagua mirror inside.

Just as on the outside, interior stairs need to have risers. If you absolutely cannot install risers of any sort, then you need to give chi a reason to want to go upstairs. It is essential that chi circulate throughout all of your home. Do whatever is in your power to create a vibrant visual flow up to the next floor. Do not forget the power of bright color.

Stairs in the center of the house are not a good idea according to feng shui, especially spiral stairs. Stairs are considered spiral if they curve around enough so that some steps are directly above other steps. They're cute, but they can easily cause a slight disorientation. If you have them, you probably cannot do anything about them, so the best idea is to bless them, hang a crystal, windchimes, or mobile over them and go on with your life.

CLUTTER

Clutter has an immediate and drastic stagnating effect upon chi. Places with dusty unused clutter that have been around for decades are about as energetically healthy as a fetid swamp. If your clutter is severe, take some severe measures. It is blocking your progress in life and affecting your health. Everything you own (even if it is in storage elsewhere) is connected to you energetically. If it isn't used on a regular basis, it's holding you back and weighing you down. Feng shui emphasizes purging clutter because the effect is so immediately liberating. The Universe cannot pour fresh new energy into your "cup" if it's constantly full of old stuff. It is virtually impossible for a cluttered place to be a clean place, and cleanliness is vital to feng shui. When it comes to reaching your potential, a dirty house is directly and strongly working against you. Faced with clutter overload, there are two preferred areas to begin clearing the clutter— near the entrance door and the Fortunate Blessings area. (See Illustration #4 and Chapter 3, Introduction to the Bagua, for an explanation of their location.) Another name for the Fortunate Blessings area is Intention, and if it is your intention to declutter, the effect will be more resounding in that area. Clutter itself is a vicious cycle, and by decluttering near the entrance of a room the stagnant inertia is broken and fresh energy can begin to flow more easily into the space, assisting the organizing process. Do not let clutter be reflected in a mirror because it is doubled.

The key to successful decluttering is to be able to pull yourself out of the emotional attachment. Here are some ways that might be helpful:

- As you are going through your objects, rate them: one, two, or three. One is for things that you use consistently or love too much to even consider getting rid of. Three is for things that you are sure you can part with. Two is for things that you can't decide about. With this technique, the things that you can't decide about don't bog you down and drain your energy. They just go into a pile, quick and easy, and you can come back to that pile when you have the energy. That way decisions get made and at least some stuff can be eliminated immediately. Work away at the number two pile a bit at a time.

- Pick up an object and as you look at it say to yourself, "If I saw this in a store right now, would I buy it?" This technique is especially effective for gifts that you never liked in the first place. I hope I'm not the first person to tell you that just because someone gave you something, that is not a reason you should keep it. Keep it if you really, really, like it—otherwise, let it go.

- Get together a group of objects and then divide the group in half according to which objects are of more monetary value. Keep the ones that are worth more and part with the ones that are worth less. This technique is appalling to some, but it sure does the trick of emotionally detaching. It probably shouldn't be the sole technique that anyone uses and shouldn't be used on all objects.

Any professional organizer will tell you that "because it may come in handy someday" is definitely *not* a good reason to keep an object. Conceivably, anything could come in handy someday. A feng shui consultant will say exactly the same thing, but for a different reason. If you are keeping an object just "because it may come in handy someday," you are saying to yourself (and the Universe) that when and if you *do* need that object, you won't have the means to obtain it. So by hanging onto it and you are truly, if unintentionally, promoting your own poverty consciousness. Hanging on to the objects can also stifle hope, thereby making deep peace more elusive in your life.

The sustainable economies of the future will have to be based on reuse. Otherwise the planet cannot support this vast number of humans. When you let go of items that you are not currently using, you release them into systems of reuse, and are helping to preserve resources and the environment.

Interior objects are functional and/or decorative. Do not over-decorate your home with nonfunctional objects—things that just sit there and look nice. It is quite important to be able to detach (emotionally and physically) from objects that are basically dragging you down. You have an opportunity to make your life better by letting go of any of these things that may be around your home:

- Representations of bodies with missing body parts or representations of ruins. See Chapter Eight: Other Considerations, page 125.

- Things that are "too unfriendly" poison-arrow-wise. See the section on Chi Flow earlier in this chapter, page 27.

- Objects that are waiting for repair. It is quite okay to have things that need a bit of repair work, but it is *best* to store them out of sight.

- Glass tabletops (unless they are rimmed) and glass shelves (unless they are over head height). See Glass Tabletops, page 115.

- "Too much stuff," which can often lead to a seemingly insurmountable messiness. Sometimes "too much stuff" means that every surface is over-decorated. Feng shui's view of having too much stuff is that you are only hurting yourself. Greed brings with it a karmic consequence, causing your life to seem too busy—no time to enjoy life. Too much stuff equals unnecessary burdens—a simple and accurate equation. If, as time goes by, you find that time seems to be speeding up, I guarantee that you will benefit by getting rid of many objects that you don't regularly *use*. Pare down your life to things you use and/or love.

We humans are adroit at making objects and have been doing so for many millennia. Don't be surprised that when you get rid of objects that aren't helping in your life, better stuff comes your way, as you are also more attuned to noticing it. The things around you *are influencing you.*

EMPOWERED POSITIONS

As chi enters a room, it brings with it the aspect of that which is new or just coming into your life. On a practical level, if you can see the main door to a room from the place where you spend the most time in that room, you've got an advantage. If you can't, you've got a disadvantage. When you can see the doorway (without moving your head more than ninety degrees), you've empowered yourself and strengthened your own natural ESP. When you can't see the doorway, you've disempowered yourself and set yourself up for surprises that you may be unprepared for. Things will seem to come out of "left field." These are the places where it matters the most:

BED

Your bed is the most important place in your home because, on average, people spend a third of their lives there. The more time spent in a particular place or room, the more resonance it has in your life. There are rules upon rules when it comes to placing a bed. Being able to see the doorway is just one of them. Others include:

- Don't place the bed so that the head is on a wall with a toilet on the other side. If this must happen, at least place a small mirror behind the bed, facing the wall, to repel the toilet vibration. The mirror does not have to be visible. Because the mirror is hanging backwards, it will not look strange because it will not be seen.

- Don't place your bed (especially your head) right next to a window, unless the window is several feet above the bed.

- Don't place a bed in the direct pathway of the door. If you have no alternative, place a screen or a large plant between the door and the bed.

- There is a Chinese custom of removing dead bodies from a room feet first, which causes some people to believe that it is unfortunate to sleep with one's feet pointed directly at the bedroom door.

- If a couple sleeps in the bed, it is important that one person does not have to crawl over the other to get out of bed. Try to have at least eighteen inches on either side of the bed for walking around.

When all these rules are applied, it sometimes leaves only one obvious place for the bed. But sometimes there is no ideal place for the bed, in which case a mirror may be needed so that the door is easily visible. Locate the mirror so that anyone in the bed can open their eyes and easily see the door. Mirrors in the bedroom are loved by some feng shui teachers and loathed by others. All agree that it's fine to use a mirror to see the door. A wall of mirrored closet doors can definitely make for disturbed sleep for some people. If that seems to be the case with you, put up a rod over the mirrors, hang curtains, and close them at night.

DESK

Your desk can be a very important area, depending upon its frequency of use and what type of work is done there. Running a business from your desk causes it to be extremely important. You need to be able to see the door from your desk without moving your head more than ninety degrees. If you are looking at a computer monitor and someone is quietly standing in the doorway waving, you need to know about it. Once again there are a lot of rules about positioning a desk. There should not be a window directly behind your back. A wall gives you support and that symbol translates into the effectiveness of the work that is done at the desk. If a window is absolutely the only option, it needs to be well screened. Shoji screens are ideal because they feel architectural. Shades and curtains are okay, but blinds can be problematic depending on how they are positioned. They need to be fairly well closed if they are behind your back. If shelving is located behind your back, it needs to be enclosed within doors so that you don't normally see the actual shelves. If this isn't feasible, just put a real "from the earth" crystal (not a prismatic lead crystal) on each shelf, from the floor to top-of-head height. Shelves that are higher than head height are problematic for a different reason. Their height is said to cause neck problems. Blinds and shelves can send out poison arrows, stabbing you in the back. There is not universal agreement about whether a desk should be freestanding in the room or be adjacent to a wall. Those who like it to be adjacent to a wall cite the concern that the desk is in a position similar to a coffin at a funeral, where it is possible to walk all the way around it. Others view the actual energetics of the desk and say that realistically it gives you more options and therefore you will *have* more options—not bad at all. If you must place a desk so that you cannot see the doorway, you will need a mirror so that if there is movement in the doorway, you will instantly know about it. Gooseneck shaving mirrors are a solution because they can be easily positioned correctly. Some people put mirrors right on their computer monitors because that's where they are looking most of the time. Small round mirrors can be attached with double-sided foam tape. It may require a bit of extra tape on one side to position it so that the doorway is exactly in view. More information on desks can be found in the section on Home Offices, page 105.

STOVE

The stove is an undeniably powerful object. If left unattended at the wrong time, it could destroy your house. When working at the stove, you need to be able to see the doorway. If it is not already set up that way, you probably cannot move it, and once again a mirror is needed. The mirror should be placed so that the cook is aware of any movement in the doorway. Mirrors behind a stove are an area of disagreement among feng shui teachers. Some modern teachers say that a mirror behind the stove is always a good idea because it symbolically doubles the burners on the stove and thereby suggests that you are able to feed more people, hinting at more prosperity. Traditional feng shui teachers say this is a gross misreading of a basic rule. The rule is that it's a great idea to have a mirror reflecting the dining room table because when the bounty on the table is "doubled," it is beneficial to your prosperity. They use the phrase "fire at heaven's gate" to refer to mirrors behind the stove and say that it portends accidents in the family. Common sense says that a mirror behind a stove is going to require a lot of cleaning, otherwise it's going to look bad. My suggestion is to put a mirror behind a stove only when it is needed to see the doorway, and try to angle it so that the burners are not reflected. A shiny stainless steel water kettle kept on the stove will serve the same purpose because of its reflective quality.

Remember those three items: the bed, the desk, and the stove. They are acknowledged by all feng shui schools as having great importance *because they can orient your awareness* of what will be happening in your life. The psychic result could be described as a gentle harmonizing with your intuition. You are willingly setting yourself up for reality. You are *aware* of the entrance and are feeding that information to your intuition. Before one moon cycle (about twenty-eight days) some part of you will have breathed a sigh of relief. Your intuition will be more grounded in reality and you will be more inclined to listen to it. Your deepened bond with your intuition is one of feng shui's greatest gifts.

OTHER POSITIONS

Besides the bed, the desk, and the stove, several other areas can have a very strong impact.

Most people have a dining table, even though it may not be used for every meal. *Wherever you sit down to eat,* you need to be able to see the doorway (and preferably not have your back to a window). Wall mirrors can sometimes help and they have the advantage of symbolically doubling the prepared food on the table. If one person in a couple always sits with their back to the door and the other person always faces the door, this sets up a dynamic which will not be healthy for the longevity of the relationship. Switch around occasionally. If there is a problem of strife (involving children) in your home, be aware of who sits where when the family eats together. The adults should always sit in the seats where they have the best view of the door. This practice will support their parenting skills. If one of the children is overactive at the table, that child should definitely have their back to the door. You can bring more harmony to dinner parties by using this principle. Place the more shy and reserved people so that they can see the door. Place your most outgoing guests with their back to the door.

If you have *a favorite lounge chair or preferred sitting spot* for reading or television viewing, you need to be able to see the doorway from that place. Either rearrange the furniture or place a mirror so that you can see the doorway.

The tub is important, but only if you take a lot of tub baths—three or four times a week. On most tubs, the end away from the faucet is the head end. That end should be farthest from the door. Then you can see the door. If your back is to the door, you will need a mirror above the faucet area, showing the door. Suction mirrors for tile walls are common. If you take long, soaking baths for the sake of relaxing, the mirror will allow the relaxation to reach deeper. Be sure not to use multiple mirror tiles, because they break up your reflection.

POISON ARROWS

In any of those six important places (bed, stove, desk, dining table, lounge chair, tub), it is best not to be in a direct line with the doorway, because the chi often comes into a room with a lot of force. This is especially the case when the door is at the end of a long hallway. When chi meets up with very straight lines the results can be quite troublesome. The energy is then referred to as poison arrow (or *sha*) energy. When *sha* encounters a place where you spend a lot of time, you need to pay attention and do something about the situation. You are being adversely affected and because it happens repeatedly, your health could suffer. It is to your benefit to know what is pointing at you. These are the main causes of poison arrows:

- Directly under *open beams* is bad if they cross over your bed, a favorite chair, where you stand when cooking at the stove, or any spot where you spend a good bit of time. If they are fake beams, remove them and be happy, but if they are structural, painting them is often the best option. Make them visually disappear by painting them the same color as the ceiling. If there's some reason that keeps you from painting, you can make them energetically friendlier by hanging a crystal or windchimes over the place where you spend time. Some feng shui teachers say that the best way to deal with these beams is by hanging a pair of bamboo flutes on them. There is a special way to hang the flutes. Use red ribbon cut to nine inches (or a multiple thereof) and hang the flutes at a forty-five-degree angle with mouthpieces down and toward the walls. This red ribbon technique can be used advantageously for hanging windchimes, crystals, etc., anywhere. Sometimes beams lend themselves to having a plant (real or artificial) trail along it and perhaps twine around it. It is especially important that the lower part of the beam be covered. Another solution is to attach beautiful fabric to the ceiling, covering the beam. Uplighting, such as a wall sconce or torchiere, can counter the effect of the beam if placed directly under it. A mirrored tabletop is a last resort solution.

- *Ceiling fans* are to be praised for their aid in air circulation, but that doesn't mean they are healthy to sit or sleep directly under. They add pressure to your life because they resemble a hand pressing down on you. They need to match the ceiling color in all situations. Sometimes this is as easy as unscrewing the blades and flipping them over. At other times, there is no choice but to paint or replace the blades. If it is possible to hang a crystal from the center of the ceiling fan, do so.

- *Adjustable louvers* are common in modern life. They come in many forms:

      —Venetian blinds

      —Mini blinds

—Vertical blinds (the worst)

—Plantation shutters

—Jalousie windows

They all have the potential of aiming poison arrows.
The main thing about them is to be sure that they are
not adjusted to aim at you as if they were blades, ready
to symbolically "slice" you.

- *Open shelves* are also considered to act as blades.
  Consider the edges of the shelves to be similar to knife
  edges and don't let them point at you. Open shelves
  behind your back are a very bad idea, especially when
  you are sitting at a desk. Move them or cover them! If
  you cannot do that, put a real earth crystal on each
  shelf.

- One of the worst poison arrow generators is *furniture
  with sharp right angles*. If the angle is well rounded or if
  it is larger than ninety degrees, no problem is created.
  However, if the angle is sharp and ninety degrees or
  less, you've got a serious situation and it's time to
  move furniture or replace it. The simplest way of
  blocking the effect of a poison arrow is to place a large
  object between its origin and its target. If none of
  these choices is feasible, there is one final option.
  Cover the offending angle with a plant, or drape
  something over it, such as a tablecloth.

To see the exact path of this kind of poison arrow, divide the offending angle in half and follow where it points. (See Illustration #2.) It is quite specific and if it points out into a space that you only walk by or rarely sit in, it isn't hurting you. The exception to that rule is: When this type of poison arrow (coming from a sharp right angle) is pointing directly at someone entering a room, it is subliminally saying "no" to them and it is also saying "no" to chi energy.

Bedside tables are truly one of the worst offenders in this category of poison arrows. Time after time I use my finger to draw a line across someone's bedspread to show where a poison arrow is going. The client gasps and says, "Oh, my God, that's where my arthritis is!" or "That crosses right over my heart. That's my main health problem." If you don't do anything else about the side tables, at least cover them (with a towel or handkerchief or whatever) when you go to bed for the night—every night. If you have extra pillows on your bed, you can use those pillows to stuff between the poison arrow and your bed. Remember, bedside tables with rounded corners never cause poison arrows.

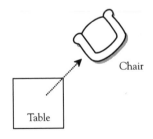

Poison Arrow from Furniture
Illustration 2

- *Doors* that are partially open can aim a poison arrow out into the room. Wherever the door is pointing in the room is where the poison arrow is pointing. (See Illustration #3.) The solution to this, of course, is to open or close your doors fully.

- *Ceiling light fixtures* sometimes have finials that point down sharply. Do not sit under them, and if possible replace them with more blunted finials.

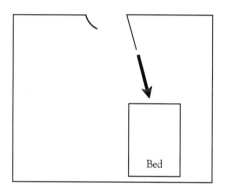

Poison Arrow from Door

Illustration 3

ATTRACTING CHI

Just as there are techniques for keeping chi out of places where you don't want it (e.g., drains), there are lots of ways to summon chi energy to certain areas of your home. For example, it is generally a great idea to attract chi to a Fortunate Blessings area.

There is an easy and very effective way to conduct chi where you want it to go. It's a trick that designers commonly use, though probably without considering its feng shui ramifications. Angle your rug. The fringe on one end of a rug says, "Step onto this end and walk off the opposite end."

When you have studied the bagua map (Illustration 4, page 59) and want to emphasize a certain area, rugs are a great way to do it. Just as they direct traffic, they direct chi. Because they are walked on, they have the quality of being fundamental, like a foundation. Angled rugs are not perfect for every situation, but they are usually fairly easy to move. Consider trying it for a week or so to see how you like it. It always makes a room more alive and dynamic.

Angled rugs and furniture are not an area of universal agreement in feng shui. Some teachers declare that angling things leads to chaotic thinking. This has not been my experience. What I have seen indicates that angling things says that the resident makes their own rules in life. The walls are there to hold up the ceiling and nothing more. They do not dictate the furniture arrangement. Realize that you can use basic design principles to your advantage. Visual energy is moved when the eye is moved in a certain way by a line or through repetition. Artists do this in pictures and it is exactly the same thing moving chi energy through your home.

There are other specific ways to attract chi. They include:

PRISMATIC CRYSTALS

These are lead crystals usually made in Austria. They are not natural stones from the earth. The round disco-ball type is often recommended. If sunlight actually reaches the crystal, you may want to use the kind that is octagon-shaped. They are unsurpassed for throwing large brilliant prisms. Crystals work in a fairly obvious way. As they move, light glints off of their facets. The more attention-getting, the more effective. Large is often best, but feel free to use any kind.

Anytime a crystal is used as a feng shui solution, it is important that you hold the intention of its use in your mind when hanging it. Feel free to say it out loud. "I am hanging this crystal to reduce conflict." The cure becomes even more effective if the crystal is hung from a red thread cut to nine inched inches or a multiple of nine inches. The crystal can hang at any height that seems good to you. It is the thread cutting that is symbolic.

WINDCHIMES

Windchimes are best if placed where a breeze can actually touch them, but don't let that stop you from putting them anywhere inside your house. If they get no breeze, just touch them occasionally to enjoy their sound. Windchimes are valued for their shape as well as their sound. The ideal shape is hollow vertical pipes, which are commonly available.

FOUNTAINS

It is hard to beat a fountain for attracting chi, because they make both sound and visual movement. One of the few places where they are not recommended is the Fame area (see bagua map, page 59), because the proper element there is Fire. Fire and water are big-time opposites! When buying a fountain in a store, be sure to put your ear right next to the motor when it is running. If the motor sound is very noticeable, you'll probably find it much more so in the quiet of your home. Many motors are almost silent, but the ones that make noise are irritating when what you wanted was water sound. Another thing to consider with fountains is the splash factor and what that may mean to nearby surfaces. A fountain motor should be turned up fairly high so that plenty of splash sound is heard. If the basin that catches the water is deep and curves up and over a bit, there will be little or no oversplash, no matter how rapidly the fountain is running. Also, something like a stone tabletop is not going to be harmed by some water oversplash, but a wood tabletop should be used with caution to avoid damage to its finish. Some fountains have a lightbulb beneath the water, illuminating the water. This is mixing two opposing elements, Fire and Water, and is not recommended. Lava lamps may be thought of in the same way.

PLANTS

Healthy living plants are obviously better than artificial ones. They don't just attract chi energy, they *are* chi energy! However, realistic artificial plants are a fine substitute in areas that are too dark or unreachable, or if the resident isn't knowledgeable about proper living plant care, or is gone for long periods of time. Feng shui cautions against plants that have the ability to hurt you, such as cactus with spines, sharp leaves like yucca, and plants with thorns. The natural defense mechanism that the plant has evolved is generally for the purpose of keeping living beings away from it. That kind of vibration within your house ("stay away") is never appropriate. (See Thorny Plants, page 155.)

DRIED PLANTS

It is best not to use dried plants unless they are less than six months old. They are dead and their energy reads dead. The sap is gone from them and they begin to rob you of your vitality and hold you in the past. Some people like to keep dried flowers from sentimental occasions. It is truly not a good idea. Strew the petals onto the ground and let them go back to the earth. Fresh energy, with your name on it, has been waiting in the wings for that moment. Artificial plants do not have this characteristic since sap was never flowing through them. Just make sure they stay clean and fresh-looking.

There is a recent design fad of using artificial flowers that look like dried flowers. They have no energy. They never had sap flowing through them, and they look dead (dried). One of the reasons that artificial flowers are such a noble craft is that it takes vibrant nature as its model. The dead version of a flower is not a desirable model. This is as true of artificial as it is of dried flowers.

CHAPTER 3

Introduction to the Bagua

One of feng shui's most powerful tools is a grid with nine areas (or guas) called the bagua (or pakua). The grid is a map that can be applied to divide a space into these nine areas, each of which corresponds to an aspect of life. The life aspect is influenced by the layout and contents of the corresponding part of the living space. This is based on the Taoist teaching of the five elements (with their associated colors, shapes, and relationships to one another) and the trigrams of the I Ching.

The elements do not refer to the strictly physical realm. They represent archetypal energies and do not stand in opposition to Western science. Many books have been written about them and much of acupuncture is based on them. Each of the nine areas has an element that is associated with it. The areas and elements are:

Life's Path	Water
Knowledge	Earth
Health and Family	Wood
Fortunate Blessings	Wood
Fame	Fire
Relationship	Earth
Children and Creativity	Metal
Helpful People and Travel	Metal
Center	Earth

There are five areas that relate most strongly to their elements. The shape that represents the element is identified with each of these five areas. These are the five areas that are not in corners:

Life's Path (Water)	Freeform
Health and Family (Wood)	Tall/Rectangular, or Square
Fame (Fire)	Angular (a pyramid or cone)
Children and Creativity (Metal)	Round, oval, or arched
Center (Earth)	Horizontal/Rectangular, Square, or Octagonal

All the areas have certain colors that relate to them. The five areas just listed have colors that are symbolized by their element. They are:

Life's Path (Water)	Black
Health and Family (Wood)	Green and Blue
Fame (Fire)	Red
Children and Creativity (Metal)	White or Pastels
Center (Earth)	Yellow, Brown, or any Earth tone

The other four areas, which are the corner guas, have colors that are arrived at by a meeting and blending of the colors in the two areas on each side. For example, the white of the Creativity area meets the red of the Fame area, making the pink of the Relationship area. Red and white are also appropriate in the Relationship area.

There are I Ching trigrams that relate to each of the bagua areas except the center. These eight trigrams are considered to be a useful Taoist tool for classifying the manifest energy of creation. The I Ching oracle consists of sixty-four hexagrams that are composed of all the possible combinations of the eight trigrams. The I Ching is a very ancient book and the translation that I recommend is *The Book of Changes and the Unchanging Truth*, reviewed in Recommended Books, page 177.

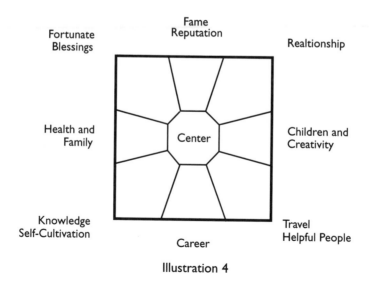

Illustration 4

CHART OF BAGUA AREAS

Area (Gua)	Alternate	Element	Color
Life's Path	Career The Journey	Water	Black and very dark colors
Knowledge	Contemplation Wisdom Meditation Intuition	Earth	Black, dark green, and dark blue
Health and Family	Ancestors Elders Community New Beginning	Wood	Green and blue
Fortunate Blessings	Wealth Empowerment Intention Abundance	Wood	Rich shades of purple, blue, and red Also green
Fame	Reputation Illumination Future Recognition	Fire	Red, Maroon, Magenta, any shade of red
Relationship	Love Marriage Partnership Commitment	Earth	Pink, white, red, and yellow
Children and Creativity	Descendants Completion Joy Pleasure	Metal	White and pastels
Helpful People and Travel	Benefactors Compassion Determination Persistence	Metal	Black, white, or gray
Center	Health Unity Tai Chi Wholeness	Earth	Yellow and earth tones such as brown, gold, and orange

SHAPE	I CHING TRIGRAM	MEANING OF TRIGRAM	COMPASS DIRECTION	COMMENTS
Freeform		Water	North	Perfect place for a fountain.
		Mountain	Northeast	Good place for books and learning tools, including television or computer or audio equipment.
Tall Square or rectangular		Thunder	East	Good place for plants and images of plants. Wooden funiture, especially tall.
		Wind	Southeast	Expensive items, things that move or shimmer. No open trashcans. Perfect place for a fountain.
Angular, triangular, pointed, conical, or uprising		Fire	South	Items related to fame—awards, diplomas. Things representing animals or made of animals—fur, bone, leather, feathers, etc.
		Earth	Southwest	Pictures of loved ones, pairs and groupings of things. No outstanding singular objects. No TV.
Circular, oval, or arched		Lake	West	Items that relate to children and/or creativity. If you have kids, the maintenance of this area will affect them.
		Heaven	Northwest	Images of deities, angels, holy people, teachers, or mentors. A good place for spiritual affirmations.
Horizontal, square, rectangular, octagonal	No trigram		Center	No bathrooms, ever! A good place for stones, or crystals, and pottery. Keep this area open and traversable.

ELEMENTAL CYCLES

The five elements relate to each other in several powerful and dynamic cycles. Upon first reading, the elemental cycles can seem overwhelming in complexity. If you are using compass feng shui (see Chapter Four, "The Bagua in Place," for an explanation), you *will* want to pay attention to the cycles and study them. Being aware of what helps or hinders your element (via the cycles) is a wise precaution. Otherwise, the chart that almost everyone should pay attention to is the "When there is too much" chart, outlined, below.

In the *creative cycle* each element is considered to give birth to the next element.

Wood   creates   Fire   (Wood is the fuel)
Fire   creates   Earth   (Ashes are as dirt)
Earth   creates   Metal   (Through time and pressure)
Metal   creates   Water   (Through condensation)
Water   creates   Wood   (Water is essential to plants)

The *destructive cycle* is not the reverse of the creative cycle. The interaction is rearranged, and the result is quite negative.

Wood   destroys   Earth   (Plants eat dirt)
Earth   destroys   Water   (The result is mud)
Water   destroys   Fire   (Quite obviously)
Fire   destroys   Metal   (Through melting)
Metal   destroys   Wood   (Axes and saws kill trees)

There is also what is known as the *conflicting (or weakening) cycle*, which is similar to the destructive cycle, but usually not as strong. It is the exact reverse of the creative cycle.

Wood   weakens Water (Eventually the water is consumed)
Water weakens Metal (Rust)
Metal weakens Earth (Metal is mined from the earth)
Earth weakens Fire (Dirt smothers fire)
Fire   weakens Wood (Wood is consumed by fire)

Both the conflicting and destructive cycles can be called upon in deciding what to do when there is too much of an element in a dwelling (or room).

When there is too much:	Add:
Wood	Fire or Metal
Water	Fire, Earth, or Wood
Metal	Fire or Earth
Earth	Wood, Water, or Metal
Fire	Earth or Water

There is a fourth cycle that is called the *mitigation cycle*. When two elements are in conflict, there is an element that mitigates the conflict. This cycle can be extremely useful in compass school feng shui, because sometimes a person's doorway is in a direction that is thought to be bad for them. The reasoning is based on the element of the person (according to their birth date) and the fact that each direction also has an element. When those two elements are in conflict, according to the *destructive* cycle, a third element can ease the conflict.

Conflict	Mitigating Element
Water with Fire	Wood
Wood with Earth	Fire
Fire with Metal	Earth
Earth with Water	Metal
Metal with Wood	Water

Various teachers explain some of the details differently, such as why Metal creates Water. If you look at these cycles and their explanations only from the point of view of Western science and logic, you are missing the point. Remember to view the elements as an archetypal energy. They are really only a Taoist metaphor for how certain energy reacts when it meets other energies.

To see what represents any of the archetypal elements, refer to the Chart of Bagua Areas on page 60. Look up "Main Element," then refer to its "Color," "Shape," and "Comments" sections.

CHAPTER 4

The Bagua in Place

This chapter describes how the bagua is used as a map to the life areas most associated with a particular part of a space. In arranging that space, you can consider that what you're seeing is a way to communicate with your higher self (or guide or guardian angel). The response back to you can seem as quick as e-mail or it can take up to a year. The average response usually occurs within a month. The way that you receive a response depends largely on your ability to notice "coincidences." That ability involves bright, open intuition and can be cultivated. When you realize that your higher self is "reading" what your living space looks like, your concept of your personal potential will, in some sense, begin to crumble. A more unlimited version will naturally take its place.

To use the bagua, imagine it enlarged and stretched to fit over your living space. An example of how a bagua is shaped for rectangular spaces is shown in Illustration #5.

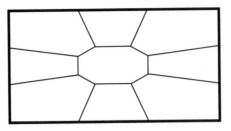

Bagua for Rectangular Spaces
Illustration 5

The grid can be laid down over the floor plan of a room, apartment, or house. It can be applied to a space as large as a plot of land or as small as a desktop. There are two very different ways to orient the bagua over a floor plan. One way is to use a compass and place the Fame area toward the south. The other way is to use the main door as the orienting factor. The side of the bagua that has the Life's Path area is laid down along the wall that has the main entrance door. Both ways of using the bagua are valid, but trying to mix the two is not a good idea. My suggestion is that if you are already drawn to astrology or numerology, then give the compass method a try. Otherwise, try the kind of feng shui that uses the entrance to orient the bagua.

BAGUA ORIENTED BY COMPASS DIRECTIONS

This method draws heavily on Taoist numerology and astrology. Humanity has evolved many systems of thought to classify people. The enneagram is one such system and Compass School feng shui is another system. In it, people are classified not only by their Chinese astrological sign (one of twelve animals) but also, and very importantly, by their element. Some practitioners also classify people by one of eight I Ching trigrams. All of these feng shui techniques are based on the person's birth time.

In using the compass method, the simple part is knowing how to orient the bagua—fame equals south—easy! (If you don't own a compass, they are readily available at camping supply stores. They are magnetic and shouldn't be placed directly on items that can be demagnetized, such as bankcards). Beyond that, things start to get complicated, because of the astrology and numerology involved (find your animal sign and element in the table in Appendix III, page 187). Once some basic calculations have been figured, you will know your element, your fortunate direction, and your fortunate number or star. The downside of this is that you will also find out that several directions are quite bad for you. If you have a spouse, their lucky direction could easily be considered somewhat deadly for you. One of the questions that arises is which direction to orient the bed, so that it can be fortunate for one of the partners. In ancient China, it was an easy decision—make it good for the guy. (Remember, this was a culture that was so terrified by the power of the feminine that women's feet were kept bound throughout their lives.) In the compass school, there aren't a lot of gray areas; things are either good for you or they're bad for you. The height of your table is either good for you, or it's bad for you—and, yes, there is a special ruler that is used to measure your furniture. On that ruler there are only two colors—one color signifying good for you, the other color meaning the size is bad for you—nothing in between. Your home gets divided into nine "magic" squares; some of those squares are great for you and others are thought to be quite terrible, with names like Death, Disaster, Bad Life, and Five Ghosts. Some people are put off by what they perceive as excess paranoia. Other folks relish the challenge and appreciate how methodical and decisive it is.

BAGUA ORIENTED BY THE ENTRANCE

For those who choose to orient the bagua by the entrance, the task is as simple as lining up the main door (of an individual room or a whole house or apartment) along the side of the bagua that has the Life's Path area. When done correctly, the Fortunate Blessings area will always be to your far left when you have just entered a room. If there is ever a question as to which door is the main door, it is usually the one close to the main entrance. Any time the obvious main door has been blocked and *is absolutely never used*, the secondary door should be used to orient the bagua.

This kind of feng shui accounts for much of its current popularity because Westerners can easily grasp the rationale behind it—basic energy movement. It is called various names, most commonly: intuitive, Black Sect, or eight-point. Since none of those names tells you much about it, for the sake of clarity I will refer to it as the entrance-based bagua.

Every time you change floors in a house (even a few steps) you set up a new bagua. The direction you are facing when you first step onto a new level is how you orient the bagua, according to the entrance method. Also please realize that there are occasionally unique houses that require bending the rules. Well-cultivated intuition is the key.

APPLYING THE BAGUA

When applying the bagua over places that overlap each other, such as a room within a house, the bagua for the individual room is most powerful. When you are in a room, that's the space that is affecting you the most at that time. Of all the rooms in a house, the bedroom is usually considered to be the most potent because, typically, a person spends a third of their life there. The more time spent in a room, the more effect it has on you. When applying the bagua by room, very small rooms, such as bathrooms and foyers, should almost always be looked at as part of the larger picture. They're a bit small to realistically lay down a bagua.

The Chinese name for an individual area of the bagua is a gua. Divide the wall of the room (or house) in approximate thirds and that will show you the location of the guas on that wall. I say "approximate" because the corner guas are actually a bit larger than the gua in the center of the wall.

There is occasionally the situation where a door is at an angle to the rest of the room. This is never a problem with the compass school. But if the entrance method is used, intuition is required once again, as well as closely inspecting the architectural details. If a door *feels* as if it aligns to a certain wall, then it does! Simple as that. If it doesn't, you can consider switching over to the compass method *for that particular room.*

When a door to a room opens directly along a left or right wall, the chi is guided by that wall, builds up speed, and then knocks into the far corner ferociously. Some feng shui teachers maintain that when this happens, the area it hits is bounced along the wall to join the area at the other corner. This means that a Relationship area could be knocked into a Fortunate Blessings area, or vice-versa. It is not a bad dynamic, it's just something to be aware of. If there is an interruption along the wall, by a large piece of furniture, the bounce is only partial. In such a case, fifty percent of the Relationship area may be left in its original location and fifty percent may get bounced. If this happened, you would just want to be sure that the Fortunate Blessings area had some of the characteristics of the Relationship area, for example, pairs of objects.

When applying the bagua over an entire house with an attached garage, the question arises as to whether or not the garage should be included in the bagua. Disagreement abounds on this issue and reputable teachers offer persuasive arguments pro and con. Some say always include the garage if the same roofline which defines the house also covers the garage. Others say that the garage is a place for parking cars—no one really lives there—so there is no need to include it in the bagua of the whole house. In my own practice, I do not usually include the garage unless it has been converted into a room and is no longer a "home for cars."

INDIVIDUAL BAGUA AREAS

Here are the bagua areas, going clockwise around a room (or house).

FORTUNATE BLESSINGS

This is always a great place to start. The *I Ching* trigram for this ares is Wind, representing the winds of change. Another name for this area is Intention. Making improvements in this area is like waving a flag to the Universe. "Hey, I'm here!" It is most commonly referred to as the Wealth area, but it is important to remember that fortunate blessings can come to you in a lot more ways than just money.

The Fortunate Blessings area provides a wonderful opportunity to prove the efficacy of feng shui for yourself. It is a very powerful area.

One of the basic things to know about this area is that *it must be clean, uncluttered, and well maintained.* If anything in this area is broken, either fix it or move it. It is great to have plants here (the bigger the better), but they must be healthy, look vibrant, and have no thorns. Two plants that I frequently recommend for this area are Dieffenbachia (Dumb Cane) and Rhapis Excelsa (Lady Palm). They are both quite easy to grow, not needing direct sun. The variegation and coloration of the Dieffenbachia leaves is quite reminiscent of dollar bills. The Rhapis is not cheap, but oh-so-elegant, especially with an uplight arising behind it.

As you might imagine, the Wealth area is an ideal place to put expensive things—things that were a stretch for you to afford. Paying more than you had planned for an object in the Fortunate Blessings area gives you what I call "the ouch factor." The symbolism comes alive in your life. It is much more real than something like a framed picture of an expensive car. Expensive things vary depending on the use of the room. In a kitchen, it would be fine to have a refrigerator in this area. In a living room or den, a television generally counts as a rather expensive object. Be aware that if the television or computer is in the Fortunate Blessings area, you *still* need to be able to see the door from your seated position. Use a mirror if necessary. See Empowered Positions, page 40.

Color is a powerful tool in all areas of the bagua and especially so in this area. Royal purple is ideal, as well as cobalt blue, and bold Chinese red. Green can also be a good color here, because Wood is the element that is associated with this area. You want rich, vibrant, saturated colors, but you don't necessarily have to get out the paintbrush. If the colors are appropriately brilliant, you don't always have to use a lot to be effective. On the other hand, don't be afraid of overdoing it. If you like the idea of saturated purple walls in your Fortunate Blessings area, feng shui applauds you.

Fountains or aquariums are absolutely perfect in this area, as are crystals. Windchimes are also excellent, since the *I Ching* trigram for this area is Wind. Garbage cans are not a good idea here, but if you must have one, it should have a lid. In the feng shui view of things, a garbage can here means you are throwing your wealth away, but a lid on it changes that dynamic. If your garbage can is in a cabinet (as they sometimes are in kitchens) it does not need to have a lid on it.

Be especially aware of the symbolism of any pictures that are in the Fortunate Blessings area. Another name for this area is Empowerment. If you have pictures of people, ask yourself if you really want those people to be exercising influence in your life.

If the windows in the Fortunate Blessings area seem overly large, you might need to hang sheer curtains to keep the chi inside. If you choose lace, use the best you can afford for this area. It is generally not a good place for mirrors because they represent windows.

FAME

This area is related to the future your reputation and what people are saying about you. Fire is the element here, and it is the meaning of the *I Ching* trigram. It is represented by red—ideally a very brilliant primary red such as is used on stop signs and fire engines. Such a saturated color is not always appropriate to add to every interior situation. If, however, you need fame in your work, I advise you to learn to love this color. Thousands of dollars of publicity will not buy what the bold use of candy-apple red can achieve if used in the Fame area. If you need fame, you cannot overdo it. For those people who just want a good reputation, tone it down. Maroon, old rose, magenta—basically any color that is in the warm end of the spectrum will have a good effect. The shape for fire is pointed, like a flame rising up. Cones, pyramids, triangles, or any shape that is sharply angular is appropriate. A few examples of this are red triangular cushions on a couch, red tapered candles, or a picture of buildings with red, pointed roofs. Fireplaces are auspicious in this area. It is the one area where I most definitely do *not* recommend water features (such as fountains) or representations of water (such as ocean pictures). It is somewhat unfortunate to have a bathroom in the Fame area, because of the amount of water involved. If this is the case in your home, you'll need to add as much red as you can stand—red rugs, red towels, red shower curtain, red soap squirter, etc. Items that represent fire, such as candles, are great here.

This area is perfect for hanging diplomas or awards, especially with red frames or red matting. This is one of the few areas where I would recommend the plant Sansevieria (Snake Plant). It has a flame-like form that almost no other plant can match. It will also grow in almost complete darkness and is as pest-free as they come for indoor plants.

Animals are considered to have the *fire of life* within them, so items of animal origin are appropriate here. Such things might be made of leather, feathers, bone, horn, fur, etc. Pictures or figurines of animals are also good. I would avoid things that come from or represent water animals in this area, such as seashells or sand dollars or pictures of fish or sea mammals.

RELATIONSHIP

The *I Ching* trigram for this area is Earth. The area is associated with all relationships, not just romantic partnerships. The most important thing to note about this area is that there should be no outstanding singular objects here. If there is a torchiere, it should be supported by more than one pole or have more than one bulb. It is best if things in this area relate to each other. There is a design concept that things are either in conflict or in conversation. In this area, they need to be in conversation. For pictures, it would be best if they were in pairs or groupings. If there is only one picture, it should have several items within it, such as a group of flowers or a couple of people. This is an ideal place to put collections of things. Anything that might represent conflict, such as guns or swords, should never be kept in the Relationship area. Don't keep kitchen knives visible within this area. Avoid fabric with stripes on it (considered to represent conflict) in this area.

Pink is the ideal color for this area. Red, white, and yellow also work. Remember the color doesn't *have* to be the dominant color, it just needs to be there someplace.

Things that have a romantic association are appropriate here. Televisions or computers are not so appropriate. They can signify a life in which that object is the main relationship. If there is no other place to have the television, it is best to cover it when it is not in use. It is also good to have something higher than the television, such as pictures, above it on the wall. Telephones are fine in the Relationship area.

Do not ever have thorny or spiky plants here. This area especially affects women and feminine energy.

CHILDREN AND CREATIVITY

If you don't have kids, this area is about your ideas and creativity, because they are basically what you leave behind when you pass away. If you do have kids, this area will always affect them, even if they are not living with you. It will also affect their offspring. If this area becomes overly cluttered, or ill-maintained, you can expect such things as bad grades on report cards. The *I Ching* trigram for this area is the Lake.

Metal is the element here and is represented by white or any pastel tones. The glint of sunlight on silver is considered to be white. Objects that have a metallic finish are also appropriate. The shape for Metal is round, with oval or arched being equally good. Creativity is associated with this element and the rounded shapes help ideas *flow*. Some objects that would be very appropriate here are round mirrors, round metal plates, trays, or pans, and lamps or pole lights that are metal and have round shapes.

HELPFUL PEOPLE AND TRAVEL

You may or may not want to travel, but everyone needs helpful friends in their life. Both of these unrelated aspects are addressed in this gua. If you are hoping to travel, or if you just want to make sure that you will have help when you need it, keep this area nice—clean and uncluttered. Pictures of far-away places are great to put in this area, as well as images of people that you think of as your mentors, teachers, or bene-factors. People who help you can be thought of as "heaven sent." Heaven is the *I Ching* trigram for this area. Images of deities or holy people would be appropriate here, as well as angels or guardian beings. Any items that have come from other lands would be helpful here. This is an area for neutral tones—white, black, or gray. This area especially affects men and masculine energy. The element that is associated with this area is Metal, so metal objects are quite appropriate here.

LIFE'S PATH

This area is sometimes referred to as the Career area, but it represents a lot more than just what you do to earn money. It has to do with your journey through life. The *I Ching* tri-gram for this area is Water. One of the most powerful things you can do in the use of feng shui is to put a representation of flowing water in the Life's Path area, since Water is the element associated with this area. Waterfall pictures are okay, but I would be hesitant to put images of huge water-falls, such as Niagara. Pictures of ponds or lakes are not ideal, because the water is basically stagnant. For the same reason, ocean pictures are out, because the water is mostly sloshing around. It is best to use pictures of rivers or streams. In this case, the water is going somewhere just by following a natural law—gravity. By representing this in the Life's Path area, you are setting up a dynamic in your own life to keep yourself on track with your life's purpose. No smacking your forehead and saying, "What was *that* year all about?"

Black is the ideal color in this area, but if that just isn't you, go for whatever dark tones appeal to you. Even dark furniture will do. Black represents water because it is as if you are looking into a deep, dark well. The shape for water is free form, like a river meandering or a drop that splashed. Items made of glass are great to use here, especially if they have a watery feel, such as glass blocks. Mirrors also represent water. The *I Ching* trigram for this area is Water and water features such as fountains and aquariums are absolutely ideal. If you have furniture like a Fifties kidney-shaped coffee table, this is definitely a great place for it.

If you are undergoing a career change, be sure this area stays clutter-free to allow fresh energy to flow in easily. Items that have to do with your career are appropriate in this area.

KNOWLEDGE AND SELF-CULTIVATION

Wisdom, Meditation, and Contemplation are other names for this area and an excellent place for an altar. The *I Ching* trigram is Mountain, and it is a great place to put pictures of mountains. Likewise, it is a good place for images of deities, spiritual teachers, and wise people. It would be best to leave out images of water unless they are on the entrance wall close to the door. This is because the element Earth is associated with this area and the mixing of earth and water creates mud. Black, blue, and green are the ideal colors, but the blue and green should be dark, navy tones. Books and other learning tools are appropriate here, including televisions, computers, and stereos. When a television is in this area, you probably have the extra advantage of being empowered because you won't have to turn your head to see the enterance. See Empowered Positions, page 40.

HEALTH AND FAMILY

The family that this area refers to is your ancestors—your parents and those who came before them. Put pictures of those people here. They are able to offer more resonance in your life from this gua. That this area also represents health is appropriate because our genes can predispose us to certain health conditions or immunities.

The *I Ching* trigram is Thunder and it is not unusual for disturbances from neighbors and the outside world to enter through this area. The best colors are green and/or blue, but yellow (and to a lesser degree, red) should be avoided or kept minimal. Yellow is the most visible of colors, is therefore "loud," and can portend even more disturbances. Fireplaces are probably not a good idea in this area. They are dealt with in the last section of this chapter.

Because Wood is the element, plants are perfect in the Health/Family area, especially trees such as ficus or palms. Representations of plants are also good—any pictures of healthy growing plants, especially trees. Wooden furniture is ideal here. Metal furniture is not so ideal, metal implements being a major destroyer of living trees.

The shape for Wood is rectangular, like tall growing trees. Square is also good. Tall, wooden furniture, such as shelves, cabinets, or armoires, is perfect to use in this area.

CENTER

Just as the Earth joins all things on this planet into a dynamic interdependence, the center of the bagua joins all the perimeter guas together. Its element is Earth, and in ancient China (and many other cultures) the center of a house was often an open-to-the-air courtyard. Here one walked across actual earth to reach the various areas of the house. The healthiest living spaces I have seen are those in which the center (of the room, house, or apartment) is open and uncluttered. It is very important for human traffic to be able to flow through this area. I once had a neighbor who lived in a small studio apartment. His bed was a folding futon, but he never folded it into a couch, preferring to keep it out as a bed at all times. The center of his apartment was *deliberately* blocked and untraversible and it showed in his life. He was constantly frustrated, floundering, and slowly getting nowhere in his life. One of the key factors here was that he had the *choice* of unblocking his Center area, but didn't. If a person creates their own problems, the consequences can be more severe, especially when they know better.

This area concerns a person's health and their ability to integrate all of who they are into a healthy personality. Earth is represented by yellow or any earth tones, such as ochre or brown. The shape is square or rectangular. Pottery, stones, natural crystals, and beautiful sand are all ways to bring real earth into this area. Fountains and other water features are not recommended in the Center because the element is Earth, and when Water and Earth are together, the result is mud. This is also the reason there is a caution about water in the Knowledge area.

There is no *I Ching* trigram for the Center.

BATHROOM LOCATION

The location of the bathroom can make or break a house more than any other room. Every school of feng shui agrees about this—don't have a bathroom in the center. This means that you shouldn't have a bathroom that is enclosed within a house. It must touch an outside wall. If you can walk in rooms of your house all around the bathroom, it counts as being in the center. Do not ever buy a house like this! Throughout humanity's history, toilets have been outbuildings. It is only comparatively recently that they are located under the same roof as the living space. To bring them into the *core* of that space just doesn't work energetically! I have known the histories of some of those buildings—bankruptcy, divorce, disease, and so forth. If you already live in one, I urge you to relocate the bathroom or move. If that is impossible, here's a list of some things you can do to *partially help* the situation. They are listed in order from the most effective to the least effective. It would be ideal to do them all.

- If there is more than one bathroom in the house, do not use the center one. Guests may use it. If there is a skylight, grow lots of plants so that it semms like a greenhouse.

- Mirror all the walls (including the ceiling) in the bathroom one hundred percent. I know that sounds pretty weird, but feng shui doesn't consider this to be a mild situation. A more acceptable alternative might be to cover all the walls in the bathroom with Mylar (shiny side facing the bathroom) and then feel free to wallpaper right over it. The reflective film is acting as a sealing agent, keeping the bathroom vibes in that one room. Covering the Mylar will not affect its sealing ability.

- As with any bathroom, keep the door closed and preferably mirrored on the outside.

- Put a bagua mirror on the outside of the bathroom above the door.

It is also not good to have a bathroom in the Fortunate Blessings area of the house or apartment. In this case, however, there *is* a lot you can do to change the dynamic.

- The toilet lid should always be down when not in use. It is actually important to have the lid already down when you push the handle to flush.

- The door should always be closed and preferably mirrored on the outside. Hardware stores sell hinge pin closers for a few dollars. They are easy to install and will automaattically shut the door.

- Put one or two large rounded stones at the rear base of your toilet. Glue felt to their bottoms if there's any chance of damage to floor tiles. The stones act as a grounding medium. They're large. They're solid. They couldn't possibly get flushed. They're gonna stay there! The plant Sansevieria (Snake Plant) can be used effectively around the toilet to counter the "flush" vibration. Its strong uprising form very effectively says "no" to that down-and-out vibration. Place it in pots on the floor on each side of the toilet tank. Snug the pots right up against the wall and as far under the tank as they can go without bending the leaves. If your tank is out from the wall a bit, you might even have leaves coming up from behind the tank. The idea is not to have any of the leaves terribly close to the seat.

- Affix a small mirror to the bathroom ceiling directly over the toilet seat, reflecting down onto the toilet. Double-sided foam tape does the job well.

- The trash can should be hidden from view. Either put it in a cabinet or use a trash can with a lid.

- Make that bathroom the finest room in your house— fit for royalty. Spare no expense. Make it nice. It should be ultra-clean and not cluttered.

- The accessories should be purple, blue, or red—rich, beautiful tones, not pastels.

If these seven guidelines are strictly adhered to, you will have dramatically changed the situation. It will have gone from a financial "drain" to something similar to a perpetual motion money machine.

It is also a good idea not to have a bathroom visible from the front door. If that is the case in your home, keep the bathroom door closed! Place a mirror either on or above the outside of the bathroom door. If the door is not kept closed, it is thought to portend kidney or bladder problems.

When you store a plunger next to the toilet, the message is, "This toilet is frequently dysfunctional." If that really is the case, then by all means, repair the toilet and store the plunger out of sight.

FIREPLACES

Fireplaces can let chi energy flow into them and then up and out of your home. When not in use, it is preferable that they have good solid screening over them. There are three areas where fireplaces can be especially troublesome.

- Directly opposite the front door and easily visible from that door. Chi flies straight into it, then up and out the chimney.

- The Center of the house (or room) is always a big no-no.

- The Health/Family area can cause exhaustion for some people (probably those who are already prone to it). Wood is the element in this area and the purpose of the fireplace is to destroy wood. This includes even a gas fireplace.

If you have a fireplace in any of those areas, it would be a good idea to change the vibration to make it less Wood-destroying. If there are months during which it isn't used, clean it well and remove all the fireplace implements. If the fireplace is in the Health and Family area, remove most metal objects from around it. Remember, Metal is a destroyer of Wood (see Elemental Cycles, page 62). Add items that make it seem as if things grow there:

- Put real or artificial plants in or around the fireplace.

- Put pictures of growing trees around that area.

- Add a fountain right in the fireplace.

- Put seashells or other representations of water around it.

- Put pottery items around it. Pottery is made from earth. Earth and water can destroy fire and they are required for wood to grow.

Do not place a couch directly facing a fireplace unless you use the fireplace often. Angle it somewhat or place it perpendicular to the fireplace. If you're not going to be using the fireplace, feel free to ignore it when deciding where to put your furniture.

There is an interesting modern design technique for screening a fireplace. Put a large, well-framed picture on the hearth and lean it in front of the fireplace.

Wood-burning stoves do not have most of the feng shui problems of a fireplace. They seal tightly and even those with glass fronts don't tend to invite chi up and out. The small pottery Mexican stoves with an open front do, however, have the same problems as a regular fireplace, but to a lesser degree. If possible, keep a growing plant on or near your woodstove during the months when it is not used.

CHAPTER 5

Extensions and Missing Areas

One other very important aspect of working with the bagua is to make sure the entire square or rectangle of your house actually is all there. A perfect square or rectangle is considered to be the ideal shape for a floor plan. Any deviation from that should be thought of as either an extension or a missing area. Extensions (i.e., bay windows) are generally to your benefit, but missing areas can be a big problem.

Sometimes it is as obvious as day and night if a dwelling has an extension or missing area, but often it is a bit trickier than that. Different feng shui teachers use slightly different formulas to decide.

A common method is to consider whether the part of the building (or room) that extends is less than fifty percent of the total area in question. The "total area in question" is shown in gray on the illustrations in this chapter. If the building part is less than fifty percent of the total area in question, you've got an extension. Illustration #6 shows an extension. Illustrations #7 and #8 show missing areas. In these cases the building part is more than fifty percent of the total area in question.

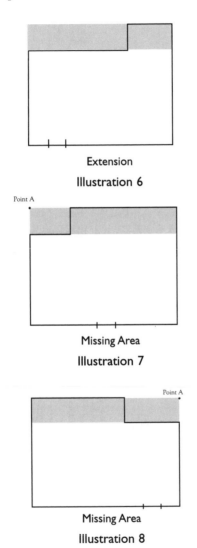

Extension

Illustration 6

Missing Area

Illustration 7

Missing Area

Illustration 8

BRINGING BACK A MISSING AREA

A mirror (the larger the better) placed on an inside wall of the missing area, facing the living space, is an effective solution. The mirror works symbolically with an "Alice through the looking glass" effect. It represents a door or window into another interior space, as it were. Also try to inhabit the missing area to whatever degree is possible—window boxes, bird feeders, windchimes. Basically try to claim the area in a way that is appropriate.

If you have a patio or porch in the missing area, place chairs there (and a table if there is enough room). Don't use it as a haphazard or catchall storage area.

If windchimes are used outside a window in a missing area, the result can vary depending on how *appropriate* a windchime is, sound-wise, for everyone who actually hears it. Do all members of a household like the sound? Do not impose loud, clanking sounds on your neighbors. Be sensitive to the proximity of neighbors' bedrooms. Disturbing your neighbors is not good sense and it is not good feng shui.

Small wind catchers are silent. Some of the wind catchers with colorful threads are so small that they can be used in almost any situation. You should see these as yet another opportunity to bring the correct shape and/or color into the missing area.

Lighting the missing area is very helpful. Strands of tiny clear holiday lights are often appropriate and easy to use. They are also excellent for giving spatial definition (i.e., you can outline your space). Any light is better than none.

Do not let your imagination stagnate when it comes to inhabiting a missing area.

Note where point A is in both Illustrations #7 and #8. It is the apex of whichever area is missing. Try to keep that apex (point A) quite accessible. If possible, do something attention-getting at that point. Frequently used items are:

- An outdoor pole lamp

- A fountain

- A birdbath or bird feeder

- A clothesline

By placing something very noticeable at the apex, you are giving that missing area some much-needed spatial definition.

WINDOW BOXES

If a missing area is above the first floor and has a window opening onto the missing area, that window is often your greatest friend for "claiming" some of that outside area. Using window boxes is almost always my number one choice, for several reasons:

You have agreed to a fairly frequent revisiting of that space, because if there are real, growing plants in the window boxes, they are going to have to be watered. You need to realize that window boxes benefit greatly from frequent watering. *Make sure the drainage is good* and that no plants are left sitting in water.

They are not difficult to install if the exterior walls are wood. Hardware stores sell special brackets made just for window boxes. If you move just fill in the holes made by the screws. Exterior masonry walls are more difficult, requiring masonry molly bolts.

They connect you to the Earth. Even if you choose to use artificial flowers in the window boxes, you are *still* more connected to the Earth than if you weren't using window boxes at all. If you are growing plants in your window boxes, you are reestablishing some of the Earth's biosystem where it was displaced or erased by the construction of your dwelling.

If you are a gardener (or are willing to learn) you can transform a lowly window box into a glorious celebration of plant life. Use the plant colors to enhance whichever area of the bagua is missing. If you are a true gardening beginner, I recommend four easy plants to get started with:

- Nasturtiums (leaves, flowers, and immature seedpods are all edible)

- Marigolds (edible flowers)

- Variegated herbs such as sage, thyme, oregano

- Any succulent with rounded leaves such as a Jade Plant or Sedum

Window boxes can be an appropriate beginning place for a larger bio-reclaiming. If you can put a bird feeder outside the window, please do so. The window box can act to catch any birdseed that is spilled (if the spilled birdseed would bother any downstairs neighbors). If a bird feeder with seed won't work in your situation, you can get an inexpensive hummingbird feeder that securely suctions onto the outside of your window.

Window boxes are a natural place to put stones and crystals. The shape and color of the stone (or crystal) can be used to enhance whichever area of the bagua is missing. A rose quartz obelisk would be ideal in the Fame area. An amethyst crystal in a ball shape or in its natural form would be ideal in the Fortunate Blessings area. Pairs of things is the principle to always remember in the Relationship area. Figurines and statues are great to use in a window box in this area, always in groups or pairs.

Window boxes can have a small-scale bagua applied to them. Larger window boxes have a natural advantage because there is a bit more space. Once again, you have the opportunity to enhance and emphasize guas that are of particular concern.

Window boxes are advantageous in many situations:

- To hide a bad view. No matter how wretched the view might have been, window boxes can change it to birds, butterflies, and flowers.

- To distract from a view that is commanding too much chi. This is any view that grabs you the instant you walk into a room. (See "Loss of Chi," page 30.)

- To bring back a missing area. (See previous section.)

CHAPTER 6

Architectural Features

DOORS

If the knob of any door can touch the knob of any other door, you have a situation known as "clashing knobs." The knobs symbolize heads butting against each other, and most likely, there will be arguments in that room or house. Sometimes it is possible to simply hang one of the doors on the opposite side of the door frame. If that can be done, the situation is one hundred percent fixed. If that can't be done, tie red ribbons or tassels from each knob that can touch another one. It's best if the ribbons are cut to lengths of nine inches or multiples thereof. It doesn't matter how far down the ribbons actually hang. I know the red ribbons can look awkward (and they don't fix the situation one hundred percent), but they're a heck of a lot better than nothing!

When a door is close to a side wall, it is preferable that the hinges be on the side of the door frame closest to the side wall. This ensures that when the door is opened, the first thing to come into view is the openness of the room.

Otherwise, the first view would be of a wall and the effect somewhat stifling.

Just as doors to rooms can cause poison arrows when left ajar (see Poison Arrow from Door, page 51, Illustration 3), doors to cabinets can do the same. Be sure to close them.

WINDOWS

Another architectural feature that causes difficulties is square windows. They have become quite popular in postmodern architecture, but they are horrible according to feng shui. If you've got them, you probably can't do anything about them, so I would advise putting up drapes, shades, or blinds in such a way that they *seem* more rectangular. If you happen to have any round or arched windows, they give your house more Metal energy and aid in creativity.

The ideal window in feng shui is one that opens fully (such as a casement window), not one that can only open halfway at a time (such as a double-hung window). Windows, like doors, allow chi to enter your life. Windows that open fully allow you to reach your potential more easily. The vitality of fresh air *is* chi energy. Let it into your home. Besides all the great fresh chi, just the act of opening and closing windows brings activity into the apex of a gua. The apex is important because it is where your realm extends farthest into the world.

Windows also represent your "inner eyes," your ability to see and know what you should be doing in your life. Clean windows allow you to do that fully. One of my clients had huge double-hung windows, but they were stuck and they were filthy. She got a handyperson to unstick them, then I showed her the easy way to clean them using a squeegee (see *Spring Cleaning* in Recommended Books). A few weeks later, I got a call from her saying she was going to move. I said, "What? You just went to all that trouble!" She replied, "I have a house north of the city that I've just been renting out because I didn't know what to do with it. Now I know that I should be living there. It seems obvious now, and I feel very solid about the decision." Hats off to clean windows!

Another thing that windows can represent is children (if you have children). The doors in the house would represent adults (i.e., parents). If the total ratio of windows to all doors is more than three-to-one, you are likely to have a problem with discipline. In other words, the children rule.

POLES

From a design point of view, poles are often an awkward architectural feature. From a feng shui point of view, they represent split vision—people (or just yourself) not agreeing on what to do. Poles are usually load-bearing, so removing them is often out of the question. One suggestion would be to symbolically join them to a nearby wall. This can be done by putting screens or tall furniture (such as shelving) between the pole and the nearest wall. You now effectively have a room divider. And if that won't work in your situation, my second suggestion is to put a tall plant right next to the pole, somewhat hiding it. A split-leaf philodendron might be ideal, because it could use the pole for support. Otherwise, any tall plant would work fine.

If the pole is very large, such as a structural column, it is often recommended to put full custom-cut mirrors on all sides of it, covering it completely. Do not use mirror tiles.

KITCHENS

For most people, the layout of the major kitchen appliances is unchangeable. Range tops and ovens are sometimes installed in separate places. It is best if neither of them is in a direct line opposite the sink or refrigerator. The stove represents fire. The sink and refrigerator represent water and since water destroys fire, the area between the appliances takes on a vibration of conflict. This vibration can create a dynamic of conflict in the lives of the residents. Hang a crystal (or windchimes) between the stove and any *water* appliance that is directly opposite it.

The same conflicting dynamic can come into play when a sink or refrigerator is located within a few inches of a *fire* appliance (stove, microwave, toaster oven, or toaster). If it is a small appliance, do whatever you can to move it further from the water.

Sometimes a stove is located right next to the refrigerator. In this case, put a sheet of shiny metal (aluminum, stainless, or copper) on the side of the refrigerator to create a real and symbolic separation. If the sink, stove, and refridgerator are all in a straight line and the stove is in the middle, it is considered to portend sadness. If the oven door opens directly in line with the entrance to the kitchen, so that you can look right into the oven when it is open, it suggests that chi will walk right in and burn right up. Hang a crystal either over the stove or directly over the cook standing at the stove.

Skylights are not good directly over stoves, because the chi from the food can vanish up and out. In this case, put a crystal, windchimes, or mobile in the skylight over the stove. Imagine a very small bagua grid applied to your stove-top (using the *entrance* method). If any of the burners don't work well, look at that part of your life, and don't be surprised to see the problem echoed. No matter where the stove is located, it always represents money. Cleaning it is no one's favorite chore, but if it is cleaned well on a regular basis, your bank account will receive an energetic boost. Don't just use one or two stove burners on a regular basis. Try to rotate their use, so that they are all used somewhat equally. Other suggestions about stove placement are in the section on Empowered Positions, page 40.

Many feng shui teachers have no opinion about what sinks are made of, but stainless steel is favored by some. Gas stove tops are generally preferred to electric, because the actual flame is there, doing the cooking. There is a common tendency to over-clutter the outside surfaces of the refrigerator with magnets, giving it a "bulletin board" effect. A minimal amount of "bulletin-boarding" on the fridge is probably not a problem, as long as it is neat, current, and doesn't get out of hand. If you like to put snapshots or post-cards on the fridge, use the clear plastic holders that are magnetic on the back. If your refrigerator is in the Fortunate Blessings corner, it would be best not to do "bulletin-boarding" at all. Instead, keep the fridge front cleaned and buffed. (A very occasional application of car wax would even be helpful.) The basic idea is that the fridge surface should be easy to clean, no matter which gua it is located in.

Do not have too many small appliances stored out on the countertop in view at all times. "Too many" is a bit subjective, depending on the size of the kitchen. Anything more than three should definitely be questioned. Perhaps if you use an appliance less than three times a week, it could be stored in a cabinet. If an appliance is clean and well maintained, it aids whichever gua it is located in within the kitchen. The trick is not to have too many out in view. It is also not a good idea to have appliances that *cut*, such as can openers or food processors, in the Relationship area of the kitchen. As mentioned earlier, open knife blades are a bad idea in this area as well. Cutting implements in a Relationship area can bring that dynamic into your relationships.

If a bathroom is located directly over a kitchen, a small mirror should be affixed to the kitchen ceiling. It should reflect downward and it should be on that part of the ceiling that is directly under the bathroom. If you are able to be even more specific, locate it right under the toilet.

HOME OFFICES

Home offices are best located in the front part of the house. The front half of a house partakes of a "come and go" energy, and offices benefit from that. Be careful that your desk is not overly large. Desks with very large surface areas can tend to "call in" that much work to do and you may find yourself much busier than you want to be. This is definitely a case of "be careful what you ask for, because you're going to get it." When working at your desk, be careful not to set pens, pencils, and scissors in such a way that they point at you.

The bagua grid can be applied to your desk using the entrance method. Where you sit is the entrance and the far right corner is the Relationship area. Do not put things that cut in that area, such as scissors, letter openers, and staplers. Telephones are very appropriate in the Relationship area, as well as a photo of you and a loved one or a photo of several people you are close to (e.g., a family photo). This is also a good area for a stack of letter trays, symbolizing relationship. If your work involves creativity, do have at least one round or curvy object on your desk, preferably in the Creativity area. There is not much you can do in the three entrance guas (Knowledge, Career, Travel) of a desk. Those areas are usually very work-intensive. If, however, you can place a large black writing pad in the middle close to you, it will help to keep you on track. The far left corner is of course very important, because it is Fortunate Blessings. Things that would help in this area are a plant or flowers, a

blue, purple, or red object such as a paperweight, or anything expensive such as a computer.

BEDROOMS

Bedrooms are best located in the back part of a dwelling because of the more restful energy there. Also, for the sake of preserving restful energy, a bedroom should only have one door connecting it to the rest of the house.

It is usually preferable to locate a child's bedroom in other areas than the Fortunate Blessings area of the dwelling. Another name for this area is Empowerment and if the children are too empowered, they'll rule the roost. If having a child's bedroom in this area is unavoidable, try to have a picture of the parents visible in that room. If a bedroom is located directly over a garage, on the next level above it, those who sleep in that room may not be getting their best-quality sleep. Some things that can aid restful sleep in this situation are:

- Put very heavy solid objects on the floor of the bedroom. Two examples would be a sculpture or a table supported by marble.

- Hang a crystal over the car in the garage. Yes, this can be done even if the garage door opens upward—just use ingenuity.

- Put a mirror (any kind, any size) on the ceiling of the garage, reflecting the top of the car.

If a bedroom is directly behind a garage, there is a similar problem, since the "metal beast" is pointed directly at a sleep area and undue pressure could be felt in that person's life. Place a bagua mirror on the back wall of the garage, so that it reflects the front of the car away from the bedroom. In both situations involving bedrooms and garages, there is not a problem for sleepers if cars are never parked in the garage.

Bedrooms that extend away from the bulk of the house in a somewhat *solitary* way indicate that whoever sleeps in that room may not feel wholly connected to the rest of the household. Put a mirror on the bedroom wall that is adjoining the rest of the house. The mirror should face into the bedroom. This will symbolically draw that room back into the house.

If a kitchen is located directly over a bedroom, it is recommended that a small mirror be placed on the ceiling of the bedroom, reflecting down. The mirror symbolically seals off the bustling kitchen vibrations from the quiet bedroom. The mirror can be tiny; even one inch will work.

There should always be a door between the bedroom and the bathroom. The door should always be kept closed at night when sleeping. That "moist" energy should not flow around you in your dreamtime. There is an architectural fad that was popularized by the so-called "monster homes." Bedroom suites are thought to be luxurious if there is no door between the sleeping area and the bath area. If you own such a home, put in a solid (not louvered) door. If that cannot be easily done, put up curtains, even sheers. The curtains can stay open until you are ready for sleep.

Feng shui does not recommend having a television in the bedroom. If you truly have no other place for your television, I suggest that you place it within a cabinet that can be closed or else drape fabric over it when it is not in use. This will symbolically close the eye of the television it off is not enough. If the bedroom is for a couple, it would be best if the television were out of there—period. When the television goes on, human relating usually stops.

The constantly open eyes of plush animals and dolls can be a factor in the restless sleep of many people. Because the eyes don't usually close, they are awake all night long. Pictures on display in bedrooms should also be peaceful.

Some people have no choice but to locate their desk in their bedroom. While certainly not ideal, this *can* work (from a feng shui viewpoint) if the desk area can be visually screened or curtained from the bed at sleep time. If you have exercise equipment in your bedroom, it should also be visually screened when not in use. Exercise and desk work are the opposite of "sleep energy."

HIGHRISE APARTMENTS

If you live above the fourth floor, I advise you to use a magnetic sleep pad under your mattress. You should also have some heavy, *and I do mean heavy*, objects on the floor of your home. Stone statues or tables supported by marble are two suggestions. Whatever the color of your floor or rugs, it should be a rather *dark shade*.

AIR CIRCULATION

The ideal building has good natural air circulation. If your home has areas with stagnant air, install a quiet fan. If parts of your home are much cooler than other parts and not lived in as much, install a gentle heater (such as a baseboard heater) to make the temperature more even throughout the home. Even temperature and good air circulation go a long way toward making a home support you in a holistic way.

Also, be aware of echoes in your home. They signify emptiness. Consider hanging a tapestry, quilt or other fabric to absorb some of the sound.

CHAPTER 7

Furniture and Household Objects

BEDS

The ideal feng shui bed has nothing stored under it, has a solid (probably wood) headboard and a footboard which isn't taller than the bedspread. Obviously, most folks don't have the ideal, so here's what to do. If things *must* be stored under the bed, those things should be emotionally "quiet." No old tax records, no old diaries. Clothes and bedding are rarely a problem, since they get laundered regularly, washing away old vibes. It is best not to be able to see under a bed, so use a bed skirt or something similar.

A solid headboard is helpful for anyone, but it is imperative for a monogamous relationship bed. A headboard with bars or slats says "open relationship" and can never hold a relationship together as well as a solid headboard. Be wary of headboards that have a high overhead shelf built in. Preferably, put nothing on that shelf (over your head) except perhaps plant vines twining together. Don't let the actual plant pots be over your head area—they should be off to the side.

A headboard backs you up and a footboard gives you grounding. If a footboard is not feasible or desired, do try to put something at the foot of your bed to represent grounding. Suggestions are a cedar chest, a bench, or even a dark-colored blanket placed at the end of your bed.

The only beds that should be sitting directly on the floor are beds that are designed that way, such as folding foam mattresses. Box springs and the like should always be off the floor.

A king-sized bed poses a problem to a permanent relationship because the mattress is usually placed upon two separate box springs (twin width). Because the box springs are closer to the floor, they are more fundamental. This reinforces the basic differences between the two partners. Replacing the bed with a queen-sized bed is a perfect solution, because it also draws the people physically closer together. If that isn't a workable solution for you, then get a red king-sized sheet and place it between the box springs and the mattress. Try to find a brilliant red sheet, because it symbolizes a new "blood" foundation.

Bunk beds should only be used if there is absolutely no alternative. If they must be used, do not let the structural support beneath the upper mattress (the metal links) be visible to the person in the lower bunk. Perhaps use fabric with a star pattern to cover it.

GLASS TABLETOPS

When chi is busily scooting and scurrying around your house, it would be best if it didn't run into a glass tabletop. The chi will get sliced and the effect will be to cut you off from reaching your goals and potential. If the glass tabletop has a rim around it, such as wood or metal, the slicing effect does not happen and all is well. Some glass stores will have a metallic tape with a faux finish. It sticks to the edge of the glass and doesn't work well on a sharp beveled edge. It is not cheap, but it looks quite good and can quickly make a table more feng shui-friendly.

If a table (with exposed glass rim) is very central, such as a coffee table or dining table, the effect is severe. If the table is away in some corner or if it's an obscure glass shelf, the effect can be quite minimal. Glass shelves which are higher than your head are probably nothing to be concerned about, at least from a feng shui point of view.

ALTARS

An altar is a visual representation of a person's spiruitual aspiration. Some people have no altars, some people have one, and some people have altars everywhere. If you do have an altar, here are some tips:

- Things that are very appropriate on an altar are a central image, a light source, flowers or a plant, a symbolic offering (such as water or fruit) and an incense holder.

- Try to have the central image at least as high as your heart (when standing). Many people have very low altars and often the reason is they don't have a higher table. Feel free to use a wall shelf.

- In most cases, it is a good idea to have the central image on some sort of upraised platform (a plinth). This could be a slab of stone or a wooden box, sometimes covered with beautiful material such as brocade. A plinth is a very respectful way of giving visual importance to a central image.

- Do not let your altar become cluttered. Clutter means hard to clean well and an altar should be nicely clean. It should not be a collecting place for crystals, special rocks, shells, feathers, etc. Your attention should be immediately drawn to the main image. It can then act as a powerful centering device in your life—visual teaching.

- A small altar need not have formal symmetry. One candle (on the right side of the altar as you are facing it) and one vase of flowers (on the left side) are enough to provide appropriate visual balance.

- A larger altar might have a balanced triad of images with candles and flowers on each side. At the risk of stating the obvious, I will say that the candleholders should match each other and the vases should match each other. An offering dish should be directly in front of the image and the incense holder in front of that (closest to you).

- If you are using stick incense, the incense holder should allow the stick to be placed vertically. This symbolizes your attentive attitude. A dish of sand works fine.

- If there is a mirror on the wall directly behind the altar, either remove the mirror or cover it with beautiful fabric.

- If the altar is in a bedroom, position it so that the bottoms of your feet are not pointing right at it. It is not considered respectful. If there is no alternative, then perhaps you could have a footboard on your bed.

Be aware to what you give visual importance and what it might symbolize. You can be giving an aspect of your home an "altar-like" vibe by excessively formalizing it. A common example might be the décor around some very formal fireplaces. Always note what you may be making an altar to. You may unconsciously be giving chi energy a message.

Many people like to pray and/or meditate in front of their altars. There is nothing wrong with that, but if you do, I suggest that you have another, much plainer spot where the majority of your quiet spiritual practice takes place. I recommend meditating or praying with your eyes barely open, looking slightly in front of you. Spiritual activity is a time of deep centering. A simple, clean blank wall (in front of you) serves as an admirable aid in meditation and prayer.

CLOCKS

If there is a clock in your home that isn't working, it should be repaired. It is stuck at some time in the past and is causing that same dynamic to happen to you. Even clocks in storage will have that effect to some degree. They hold you back and keep you from reaching your goals. Stoves with built-in clocks can be especially problematic, because the stove is so powerful. Very often the clock stops working decades before the stove. Of course, the best thing is to have it repaired, but if you are a renter, the cost may seem prohibitive. I would suggest using tape to cover over the clock as neatly as possible, then buying a small timer if you have been using the built-in one.

A working clock acts as an energetic boost to any area in which it is located. If the clock has noticeable movement, such as a pendulum, so much the better.

MIRRORS

Mirrors have many uses in feng shui and are frequently recommended. They indicate how truly and honestly you see yourself. They should always be clean and in good repair—no cracks, no bad silvering. A cracked mirror gives you a fractured image of yourself, as do mirror tiles. There is a recent design fad of having mirrors inside the mullions of a window frame. The only time one of those mirrors would be acceptable would be if it were placed high enough so that no one in the house could see their reflection in it.

Old mirrors with bad silvering cannot give you a true reflection of yourself and can contribute to low self-esteem. In the case of an antique, the bad silvering actually adds to the value of the piece, and if that's the reason you own it, here's what to do. Have the old glass removed, save it, and replace it with new mirror glass. If and when you sell the piece, put the bad mirror back in and the value is preserved, but you haven't had to live with the consequences of it for all those years. Incidentally, new mirror glass is incredibly cheap.

Also, mirrors of smoked or colored glass should be avoided. Some mirrors have designs etched or painted on them. It is best not to have these mirrors in your home, but if you already have one and want to keep it, put it at a height where no one can see themselves in it. If the design is just around the border, the mirror can be used anywhere.

Every adult residing in your home should be able to fully see their face when standing in front of any mirror (which is intended for that purpose). If not all of their head can be seen they may experience problems such as headaches or unclear thinking. Ideally a mirror should also show the space eight inches above a person's head, because that represents their potential.

Mirrors give the illusion of expanding a space and this property is useful any time you feel the need to symbolically enlarge a tight area. This also lets you "bring in" fresh energy to any gua in which a mirror is placed.

It is important to be aware of what a mirror is reflecting, because it is symbolically doubling that view. It would be best not to reflect clutter, toilets, or *bottoms* of stairs. There is one seemingly odd exception to mirrors reflecting toilets. Many feng shui teachers recommend putting a small mirror *on the ceiling* reflecting directly down onto the toilet. I would consider this especially important to do if the toilet is in the Center or Fortunate Blessings area of the residence.

Mirrors are able to seal off certain undesirable vibrations, such as from bathrooms. See Loss of Chi, page 30.

Mirrors can symbolically bring back missing areas. See Bringing Back a Missing Area, page 91.

Mirrors are superb for repelling menacing energy. They reflect it back on itself. See Chapter One: The Exterior, page 13.

Do not use convex or concave mirrors to view yourself on a regular basis, unless you need the enlargement for something like makeup application.

SYMBOLISM

Feng shui takes symbolism quite seriously and literally. Be cautious of these kinds of symbols in your home:

- One of the things that can affect you is *representations (pictures or statues) of bodies with missing parts*, i.e., the Venus de Milo. Sooner or later, that symbolism will begin to have a detrimental effect on your health. A statue of a head without a body may or may not be problematic. If the statue looks as if it were originally intended to only be a head, i.e., the bust of Nefertiti, there is no problem. But if it looks like it was lopped off a larger statue, it retains some of that vibration.

- The situation is much the same with *representations of ruins*. Such symbols say that your glory years are a thing of the past. It is best to part with such objects.

- *Masks* can be problematic in several ways:

    —The most obvious thing about a mask is that it is hiding the real you.

    —The expression or facial features are important to consciously recognize. Question how they represent you or your family. It may not be bad, but at least *think about* what it means.

    —If the mask is an old ethnic mask and was used shamanistically, it can sometimes have a very strong effect on people (maybe yourself?).

The overlay of vibrations because of its ceremonial use can be powerful. See Used Objects, page 144.

- *Dead flowers*, see Dried Plants, page 55.

- The simple symbolism of a home that is *visually over-cluttered* says that the life of the resident (or residents) will seem busy or hectic. See Clutter, page 35.

- Pictures of your *ex-relationship partner* should not be on display if you are seeking a new relationship. By putting those pictures away in a scrapbook you are symbolically making room for someone new.

- A drain is a drain is a drain. It can drain energy and money out of your life. See Loss of Chi, page 30.

LIVING ROOM FURNISHINGS

When arranging the main furniture of the living room, it is important not to put seats *directly* across from each other. It would be better to angle them somewhat. Directly facing each other can say "opposing positions" and create disharmony.

If the living area and dining area are together in one large undivided room, it's time to think about a room divider. (An L-shaped room counts as an undivided area.) The divider should preferably be solid, like tall shelving, cabinets, or decorative screens. If that won't work in your situation, try a couple of tall plants, graciously announcing the entrance to the dining area.

CHAPTER 8

Other Considerations

YIN/YANG

In computer language, it's either zero or one. In Taoism, it's either yin or yang. Just about everything imaginable can be divided into these two. If it isn't divided hard-line, it is somewhere on a scale between very yin and very yang. Some of the concepts that apply to interiors are divided thusly:

Yin	Yang
Lower part of a room	Upper part of a room
Private	Public
Moist	Dry
Dark	Light
Complex	Simple
Female	Male
Cold	Hot
Soft	Hard
Quiet	Noisy
Indoors	Outdoors

Following this logic, a bathroom is a very yin room. It has no stove or oven to help balance the several areas of wetness (tub, shower, sinks, and toilet). If a bathroom is visually busy or complicated, the yin component is pushed off the scale and the room becomes very out of balance and less healthy. To alleviate this, keep it simple—almost to the point of austere. A bathroom can be elegant and feel wonderful if you simply use color as the uniting theme. Use the appropriate bagua colors, depending on where the bathroom is in the house. Bring those colors into the room through the towels, bath mats, shower curtain, soap dish, or soap squirter. Laying down a bagua for a regular-sized bathroom is a losing proposition. The space is really just too small to make effective statements for each of the nine guas. Instead, if the bathroom is in the Creativity area of the house, go for chrome and pastels. If it is in the Relationship area of the house, go for pinks, reds, and whites, and groupings of things. The bathroom is often decorated with water imagery—seashells, pictures of the ocean, etc. Once again, this makes the room too yin. Only if a bathroom is in the Life's Path area would I recommend *any* water imagery—preferably a picture of a flowing stream or river. If the bathroom is in any other part of the house, do not add water imagery to an already wet room.

Note that yang is public and yin is private and quiet. A home is naturally a more yin place than a store. However, a home can be too yin (or have parts that are too yin—see Guests, page 133). Examples are:

126

- A home that is directly next door to a building that is not well used on a daily basis (i.e., churches).

- A home in which a pet is left alone all day and the animal spends many of its hours listless and somber. That vibration continues to affect the dwelling.

- A home with a bedridden person.

MOVING

The first step toward a new home is often to improve the home you have now. "Bloom where you are planted" is a wise adage. Time after time I have seen someone make a dump look just gorgeous. Then, out of the blue, the opportunity arises to move to someplace much nicer. It is as if the Universe were saying, "Well, you did a great job on that one. Let's see what you can do with this one." Give a word of thanks for your old home, regardless of how grateful you may be to be leaving it. It sheltered you.

Directionology is a particular aspect of feng shui that only affects a person who is moving residences. The charts for figuring the best time for a permanent move are in Sarah Shurety's *Feng Shui for Your Home* (see Recommended Books).

LOCATING A NEW HOME

Absolutely everyone is intuitive to some degree. Even if you don't normally think of yourself as intuitive, when you are deciding which new home to live in, be very aware of how you *feel* about the neighborhood as you approach a potential new home for the first time (and any time thereafter). When I say "new home," I'm referring to *new for you*. Building a new house, or buying a brand-new house are not feng shui prerequisites for a fabulous life. It does not matter if you buy or live in a new home or a used one. Many period homes (pre-2000 A.D) have excellent feng shui energy.

Because of burgeoning population, new suburban construction is occasionally built over poorly marked private cemeteries. There are no federal laws in the United States that protect abandoned cemeteries on private property. Local statutes are often inadequate and sometimes unenforced. To all new homeowners, my first advice is to do a Space Clearing. (See Vibrational Cleansing, page 140.)

These are major deciding factors when deciding which home to buy or live in:

- Do not buy a house with a bathroom in the center unless you are willing to have it removed before you move in. Period. (See Loss of Chi, page 30.)

- Steps going up to the front door of your new home must have risers. (See The Exterior, page 13.) If risers can be installed, there is no problem—just do it ASAP.

- When you step inside the front door, make sure there is no missing area in the far left corner of the residence. This is considered to be a powerful area by all feng shui schools. If there *is* a missing area there, and you still feel that it is your best choice, go ahead. You must, however, be willing to bring back that missing area to the best of your ability. (Suggestions are on page 91.) If not done quickly, the new home risks being thought of as a money pit.

- Even if you have no choice about which direction you will move, you should still consult a table of Directionology. (See previous section.) To be forewarned is to be prepared.

- Consider how the element of the house relates to the element of the landscape. The elements of the house and landscape are based upon their shape—primarily their profile as you approach them. The explanations in *Simple Feng Shui* are quite understandable. (See Recommended Books.)

REPAIRS AND RENOVATIONS

REPAIRS

Repairs and renovations mean very different things to renters and to homeowners. Not every owner of rental property is conscientious. If you are a renter, please be assertive when repairs are due to your home. Be the squeaky wheel that gets the oil! Note the area of the bagua that is in need of repair. That aspect of your life is probably "getting clobbered."

It would be nice if all windows opened fully, but many are painted shut. The importance of fully functioning windows is discussed on page 99. Unstick those windows, even if you have to hire someone. Do this even if you are a renter! You're the one living there—you will receive the benefit.

RENOVATIONS

The feng shui view of major home renovation is that you are operating on a body. Proceed with care. The results can be great or horrible. I recommend talking to the space that is going to be disturbed, explaining what is going to be done, and why. Give it advance warning, and perhaps say, "You'll like it" or something similar.

When creating additions to your home, it would be best to "fill in" any missing areas. There is no universal agreement in the feng shui world as to which is better, an addition making a house deeper or an addition making a house wider. (See Illustration #9.) I almost always recommend deeper, because it adds depth and resonance to the occupants' lives. By making a house wider, you are increasing people's ability to be further removed from each other (and they will be). Never make the second floor of a house seem larger than the first floor, as this can bring an instability to its residents. Viewed from the front, a house should look balanced, left and right. Renovations can create or accentuate that "balanced look." If you have the opportunity to create a "bulge" in your Fortunate Blessings area, do so. You will never look back! When a new space has been created within a home, I recommend singing or chanting within that space to welcome it, energetically connecting it to the rest of the house.

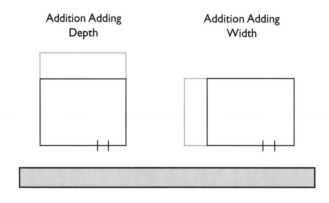

Illustration 9

GUESTS
YOURSELF AS A GUEST

- **Hotel** If you are staying in any form of public lodging you can easily make your stay more feng shui-friendly. Ask for your room to be in the rear half of the facility and away from elevators. Just before going to bed, cover any and all poison arrows that are aiming at the bed (see Illustration #2, page 50). I recommend covering them just before going to bed (towels are fine) and removing the covers as soon as you rise. That way your place doesn't look weird. A television only needs to be covered when you are sleeping, but feel free to cover it any time you want. The bathroom door should be closed when you are sleeping.

- **Staying with friends** If you are staying with friends, exactly the same principles apply, except that you probably won't have a choice about the location of the guest room. Do be sensitive not to inadvertently offend your host as you make your place more feng shui-friendly. Remember, poison arrows that aim at a bed only have to be covered while you are in the bed. Receive your guest lodgings with gratitude. Feng shui highly approves of the old courtesy of expressing your appreciation by sending a "thank you" card when you have arrived home.

GUESTS IN YOUR HOME

- **If you have a guest room** in your home, but it is seldom used, it may be too yin. Any room can become too yin by being underused/under visited. Notice where the guest room is in the bagua of your whole house. The corresponding area of your life may be rather inactive. The best solution I know of is to simply *use that room*—do *something* in there on a regular basis. A small decorative light on a timer to come on for a few hours in the evening is another option. If your guest room also doubles as an office, which is increasingly popular, cover the unused computer screens while a guest is staying in the room. A nice fabric, perhaps.

- **If you don't have a guest room,** then plan so that your guest's possessions don't clutter any guas that you are working on. My friend Sally let a friend stay with her for a week. Sally was living in a very nicely maintained studio apartment, and she knew enough about feng shui to know where the different bagua areas were. But without thinking she let her friend's things go into the Relationship area of her apartment. During that one week, Sally said that basically all the relationships in her life "fell apart," resulting in her moving away. One of the best ways to make a guest feel welcome is to provide horizontal space for them to put their things, such as tables and drawers. Such a place would ideally:

—Feel secure and somewhat private

—Not be in the Fortunate Blessings or Relationship guas

Occasionally think of yourself as a guest in your own home. Do be grateful. At some point in time you will permanently leave your dwelling. Rare is the person who is born and dies in the same house. In a sense, we are all visitors to the dwellings that shelter us. We should endeavor to leave them cleaner and nicer than when we arrived. Otherwise we probably accrue some "bad karma." Treat your home well—maintain it and keep it clean. If you can train yourself to develop the ability to *truly* see your home as a visitor might, you've gained a valuable feng shui skill.

PREGNANCY

It is commonly believed in feng shui that if a woman lives in the same house throughout her pregnancy, the child will easily settle down for very long periods of time. This has nothing to do with how soon they move away from their parents. If a pregnant woman changes homes, the child will probably have a bit more of what we might think of as "gypsy blood." Settling down will not come as easily or naturally for that offspring.

Some feng shui authors offer a formula for getting pregnant. See *Feng Shui: Harmony by Design* in Recommended Reading. One of the recommendations is that you refrain from cleaning under your bed while trying to become pregnant.

THE NUMBER FOUR

There is absolutely nothing wrong with the number four. You may have heard that some Chinese people consider it to be an unlucky number. That is only because the sound of the Cantonese word for "four" sounds like the Cantonese word for "death." That is a very linguistically and culturally specific thing and has nothing to do with the energetic power of four. It is a strong number and a foursquare building is considered *ideal* in feng shui.

The sound of words that are in a language that you (perhaps) don't even understand means zero to you. Whatever your house number is, find a reason to like it. See it as a strong number.

ORGANIZING

Feng shui views organizing (and cleanliness) as *kindergarten*. They are basic—fundamental. I truthfully stress their great importance. It is near impossible to reach your highest potential and achieve your goals without organizing and cleanliness. Develop organizing skills. There have been hundreds of books written on organizing, but disorganized people are often the last ones who have time to read them. Audiotapes are more accessible—everybody has time to listen to a tape. You can listen while in transit or when bathing. I believe that the very best information on organizing is on Stephanie Winston's audiotape *Getting Organized* (see Recommended Books). Listening to this tape several times can probably cure anyone's disorganization.

Don't put obstacles in the way. Prioritize your time. You may have to be diligent to keep this as one of your very highest priorities. If your abode looks helter-skelter, it is not supporting you to your highest potential. It is as simple as that!

Think of everything in your space as information. That information is being heard by you and your higher self. (Please substitute whatever words feel more appropriate to you—guardian angel, guides, Universe…). What you *don't* want to be hearing (consciously or subconsciously) from that information is, "Come here! Go there! Do this! Do that!" You also don't want to be hearing, "Don't look here," which is what you can be unconsciously saying to yourself and others when you honestly look around the room and see things like:

- Jumbles of electric cords (signifying a confusion of power)

- Clutter

- A look of "Oh, this hasn't been cleaned in quite a while."

Chi looks everywhere and at all details.

The one-list method is the most surefire way to see (and not just wonder) what needs to be done in your life. It should be a totally *active* list. You write things down, and then cross them off when you've done them. Draw from your one main list, kept in one place (such as a small six-ring binder), to put items on a daily list. Use a calendar for writing appointments and reminders in the same small binder. As soon as you've *written* something on a list, its psychic "voice" is quite muffled. You are no longer hearing, "Do this! Do that!"

Your home should be giving you a big dose of visual serenity and should support you in practical accessibility. Frequently used things need to be very easily accessible. Adhere to the rule that if a shelf or drawer is at an accessible height for you, its contents should primarily be things that you use often.

VIBRATIONAL CLEANSING

One of feng shui's greatest gifts to the Western world is its acknowledgment of unseen energetic vibrations. In the feng shui worldview, this acknowledgment is understood as basic common sense. Such vibrations can belong to single objects or they can be hanging around an entire house. If a house or object had previous owners, there's a fifty-fifty chance that it has picked up some vibes. There is also a fifty-fifty chance that those vibes are excellent and to your benefit, so there is no need for undue paranoia. There is, however, the slight chance that something that was previously owned has picked up vibrations that are not particularly good for you, a sort of "psychic dirt." Once again, there is no need for alarm. Just use incense or a smudge stick to cleanse the old vibrations. The vibration, or residual energy, of previous oc-cupants can be mild or heavy. Everyone can sense it to some degree (although some people have cultivated the ability more than others). If it is an entire residence that you feel needs cleansing, sometimes called space clearing, here are some tips:

- Do it during the day.

- Have every window open as fully as possible. Let the natural breezes do some of the work for you.

- If the place is physically dirty, do a thorough, detailed cleaning of the entire space in conjunction with the vibration cleansing. If possible, do the physical cleaning first.

- Walk the entire inside perimeter of each room, including closets. Go in a clockwise direction, which means turning to your left as soon as you have entered the room.

- Carry burning incense or a sage smudge stick.

- If you can manage it, carry a pure-sounding bell, and ring it every few steps. If someone is assisting you, one can carry the incense and the other can carry the bell.

- If no bell is readily available, don't worry, you were born with the right tool—use your hands and clap. Don't clap as if you were applauding. Do single, loud, sharp claps when you get to corners and doorways and any place that feels a little unusual—any kind of unusual. It is an extremely powerful, assertive thing to do. You are using your own hands to claim your rightful ownership of a space. Clap high and clap low. There is no way that you can clap and hold incense at the same time, so if you are doing this alone, you will have to make two complete circuits. If you have time, go ahead and make a third circuit. Three is a very powerful number.

- Sing, chant, or speak aloud—whichever you are most comfortable with. The ancient chant "Om" is always appropriate. Absolutely anything that expresses your intention is appropriate. You could simply say, "Peace to this space," over and over. Your voice should sound assertive and be rather loud. Don't worry about the neighbors. This is most likely to be a one-time occurrence, and even if they can hear you, they'll get over it.

- Make sure the smoke from the incense wafts high and low. Bring the incense near the floor and the ceiling, in every corner, including closets and cabinets. Do an ultra-thorough job. It's okay if it takes a while. You are not going to be doing it every day.

If, after doing all this in your home, you are still concerned because of unexplainable, uncomfortable feelings, it may be time to call in an expert. I'm referring to any psychic with an excellent reputation who knows how to do "ghost busting." Buddhist priests are also recommended in this regard. You *can* find someone if you set your mind to it.

When buying a house, try to find out something about the history of the previous owners. If the house is being sold due to divorce or bankruptcy, the deal may look good, but look at the property from a feng shui point of view. If you notice something that might indicate hard times, such as a missing Fortunate Blessings area or a stove and refrigerator right next to each other, you might want to be sure that you can correct the situation. Otherwise, history may repeat itself.

The first and fundamental attitude to have toward any object that you own or any space that will shelter you is gratitude. It is the basis for all true spirituality and is always appropriate (even if it is your intention to eventually move).

USED OBJECTS

Exactly the same principles that apply to space clearing also apply to object clearing. It is the vibrational cleansing of an object. You can just pass any object (new or used) through incense or sage smoke and use the sound of your own voice. Saying something as simple as, "I bless this object and welcome it into my life" has an honest directness that penetrates the Universe.

Any object can be restored to its original vibrational purity. If you don't feel confident of your ability, ask for professional help.

Every object comes from the body of this planet. Used objects have a natural ecological advantage. The planet is shared by all kinds of people, and no one is exempt from showing respect for the ecosystem. It concerns us all. Any act of compassion for the planet brings groundedness, and the blessings of the Earth element into your life.

NON-FENG SHUI TECHNIQUES

These are disciplines that evolved separately from feng shui, but are very complementary.

DOWSING

Dowsing is the ancient art of walking around holding a stick or rod which then dips down while going over water. It can be very useful to find out if there are underground streams on your property. Dowsing can also locate areas of geopathic stress that may or may not be related to a stream. Don't think that this applies only to country property. A dowser can pinpoint stream locations, even if you live in a town house.

PENDULUMS

A pendulum is a pointed object suspended from a chain or string. The direction of movement of the object answers yes or no questions. Many people like to use a pendulum to bring accuracy to questionable situations. Sometimes it is good to double-check a decision using a pendulum.

EMFs

Electromagnetic frequencies are a fact of life that ancient feng shui masters never had to deal with. There are sophisticated devices using diodes or magnets to counteract harmful frequencies. It requires no special talent to locate electromagnetic hot spots in your home. Meters for measuring such frequencies are available from ALPHALAB, 800-769-3754, www.trifield.com.

Aromatherapy

Aromatherapy is a recent name for an ancient art studied by many cultures. How a room or dwelling smells is very important. Diffusing essential oils is the most often recommended technique in aromatherapy books, as well as scented candles. Incense is also commonly used by those who don't mind the bit of smoke. My favorite technique is to grow plants indoors that have fragrant blossoms. Tovah Martin's book, *The Essence of Paradise*, is an essential reference on which plants will succeed where. Unfortunately, it is out of print. Use a search service or interlibrary loan to obtain a copy.

Vastu

Vastu (sometimes called Vastu Shastra) has its origins in the ancient Indian Vedic civilization. It is both sacred and practical, with many applications for modern dwellings. This system for designing buildings and working with space has some similarities with feng shui, yet it is "its own thing." The five elements of Vastu are Fire, Water, Earth, Air, and Space. Books in English on Vastu are not nearly as abundant as feng shui books.

CHAPTER 9

Gardening

Gardening is a basic and marvelous skill to acquire. Whether you garden indoors or out, it is a rewarding and fulfilling art to study. Plants (both living and artificial) can mute the effects of poison arrows within your home and in the landscape outside. Trees and hedges can be protective and act as guardians. The most effective guardian trees are tall and old and are best located behind your house.

LANDSCAPING

Some aspects of landscaping, primarily those dealing with the front yard, are discussed in the first chapter. The bagua is laid down over an entire plot of land, encompassing the front and back yards. If, however, the back yard is a separate space, fenced off from the front yard, it can be considered to have a full bagua all of its own. If using the entrance-based bagua map, the Fortunate Blessings area would be located in the back left corner. Don't have a compost heap there or in the Fame area. Any other area is fine. Since most folks want the compost somewhat removed from the house, there is absolutely nothing wrong with a compost heap in the Relationship area. A lot of microbial relating has to happen to create rich, healthy humus. The Relationship area is also a great place for a food garden or a clothesline. It is the perfect area for lawn furniture. Whenever lawn furniture is placed on your property, give some thought to its color in relation to that area of the bagua on your land.

When you lay the bagua over your property, note the colors that are appropriate for each area. Plants that bring in those colors are a great way to use feng shui in the landscape. Flower color is not the only way. Variegated leaf color is often more long lasting and maintenance free. Dark purple leaf color is excellent in three areas: Knowledge, Life's Path, and Helpful People.

The Fortunate Blessings area of your yard should be stunning. If it is used as an unattended catchall area for storing "junk," you've got some work to do! This opportunity should be viewed positively, since you actually have a great chance to "reintroduce yourself" to the Universe and bring in some wonderful fortunate blessings, perhaps in the form of money. If there is an outbuilding in that part of your property, it should look good on the outside and be orderly inside.

Pathways in general should vary in width in order to take advantage of their ability to "funnel" chi into a dwelling. They should therefore be somewhat wider when they are at their farthest distance from the house. This can often be gracefully accomplished by flaring the pathway where it meets a public sidewalk or any other destination away from your house. As a general rule, make all paths meander somewhat. Avoid long, straight paths, especially if the edges are straight lines. If you have such paths (like long straight cement walkways), allow the plants on each side to grow over the walkway a bit. Don't do severe edge trimming, as this only emphasizes the straightness.

If any of the statuary in your garden is spiritually significant, raise it off the ground in whatever way is appropriate and safe for the statue.

Evergreens are an important symbol in feng shui. They come in all sizes, so don't just think of them as big trees. If you live in a climate where plants drop their leaves in winter, evergreens can counter that "dead" look. Evergreen hedges are especially important because they maintain your privacy and establish your borders.

Establishing privacy is considered by many to be a number one goal in gardening. If this is feasible, go for it. It will probably mean that you will feel freer to visit areas of your yard or property where you might otherwise seldom go (especially if they are in public view). Try to spend time in, and pay attention to the feel of, each area in your yard. Start with the Fortunate Blessings area. Improvements there will be more resounding. An alternate name for that gua is Intention.

PRUNING

Pruning hedges is a straightforward chop-chop for many people and that is definitely okay unless the hedge seems quite long. A long, straight, box-trimmed hedge is never expressive of a plant's true form and can definitely cause chi energy to accelerate too much. If that seems to be the case, find some way to soften the line. Your goal (according to feng shui) is to allow your plants to "scoop up and funnel in" the chi energy that is going past your lot. Often, straight boxy hedges just escort chi energy past your property at a brisk pace. If planting a new hedge, consider:

- A relatively untrimmed hedge of mixed plantings. (Any good nursery will have suggestions appropriate to your climate.)

- A serpentine formal hedge. Not only does it most definitely slow chi energy down, it says "Wow!" if done nicely. (Note: Any time you've made something on your property that says "Wow!" you have done a primo job of pulling in chi energy.)

Other than formal hedges, all pruning should be done considering the natural growth form of the particular plant.

Pruning is an essential part of horticulture. You do it every time you remove leaves that are dying on a house plant. If you don't know how to prune like an expert, please learn. *Never leave a stub!* Those stubs are not allowing the plant to heal over the wound effectively and quickly. Until the wood is sealed, the plant is more susceptible to bugs and disease. The stubs are also potential poison arrows (depending on their size).

Make sure no trees or shrubs are *hugging* your house. It has a stifling effect on your life.

THE FIVE ELEMENTS

It is important to bring as many of the five **elements** as possible into your landscape. Try to do so in the appropriate area of the bagua.

EARTH

Use stones on walls or pathways, or to symbolize a stream bed. Bricks are also fine for walls or paths. Large boulders are excellent and were frequently used in ancient Chinese gardens to symbolize mountains. Planters and garden ornaments made of clay are another way to bring in this element.

WOOD

Every plant in your garden symbolizes wood—even grass. Trees are, of course, ideal, because the wood is real and not just symbolized. Wood lawn furniture also expresses this element.

FIRE

Exterior lighting is often the simplest way to bring in this element. If installing exterior lighting seems intimidating to you, consider using tiny clear holiday lights—"fairy lights." Also, outdoor cooking areas are an appropriate way to bring fire into your yard. Attracting wildlife (through bird feeders, etc.) is also a way to bring the "fire of life" into your landscape.

METAL

Metal garden ornaments and lawn furniture are the easiest way to bring metal into the landscape. You don't have to use both. Some people simply don't like metal chairs and that is certainly understandable. Reflective metal balls are back in vogue for gardens. The blue-colored ones are great for the Fortunate Blessings area. Outdoor metal windchimes should be used with great consideration for any neighbors who might hear them. Don't be shy about asking your neighbors if the sound is pleasant or disturbing to them. It is best to know! If you are disturbing your neighbors (even if you're not aware of it), you are attracting negative energy. If that is a possible consideration in your area, use bamboo wind-chimes or very small metal windchimes, so that the sound is more gentle. Metal swing sets or play equipment are a good option for people with young children.

WATER

Fountains, pools, and birdbaths are all fairly common ways to introduce the water element. Swimming pools also work, but a large, prominent swimming pool directly behind a house can signify an abyss. It is often recommended that the pool be visually screened from the house. A kidney-shaped pool should always have the *concave* part facing the house. The Fortunate Blessings area is always ideal for water fountains or bird baths. Flowing water symbolizes blessings flowing into your life and a pool represents a reserve of good fortune.

HOUSEPLANTS

Plants are conscious life. They can enchant an interior like nothing else. Think of your home as an *interior landscape*.

Do not have too many *drooping* houseplants—plants that hang down below their pot. This can add depression to your household. Also, do not allow plants to touch the ceiling. This says that you have reached your limit in the gua the plant is located.

It is important that a houseplant be healthy. If the plant is having a hard time and you are nursing it along, make sure that it is not in the Fortunate Blessings area.

A word about bonsai—*true bonsai* keeps a plant in the same pot for possibly hundreds of years, using wires to dwarf it. Such techniques are frowned upon by feng shui because of the stunted chi energy. Plants which are naturally small or genetically dwarfed can be charming and do not create a feng shui problem. Such plants can be used to make a miniature landscape which can include a fountain.

THORNY PLANTS

Whether the plants are grown on the exterior or interior of your home, thorns are not a good idea. Certain plants evolve thorns as a way of saying to other living things, "stay away." Just like porcupine quills, they are a natural defense. To anyone who has had painful experience with thorns, they are a symbol as understandable as a red hot stove. The message from thorned plants is for you to avoid (or be extremely cautious of) some part of your space.

When you are emphasizing a particular area of the bagua, you should realize that situations will change as time goes by. You may want to emphasize other bagua areas in a few years. All types of astrology and numerology, Asian and Western, recognize that every person's life is going to go through a unique set of cycles based on their birth time. Even though you may not feel the need to emphasize a particular area right now, you should not deliberately install a message of "don't go there." No areas of the bagua are truly expendable. Missing areas should be brought back, if only symbolically. Any area that is excessively thorny (i.e., a cactus collection) is causing you problems. The smaller the place you live in (i.e., studio apartment), the stronger this effect applies. A large plot of several acres has much more leeway because the physical size of a gua can concentrate or dilute an effect.

Plants with spiky leaves that can hurt you, such as yucca and agave, are to be thought of as thorny plants. The Fame area is the one place where I can say a reluctant "okay" to spiky plants like agave or yucca. They do have a strong up-rising quality, but they also say, "don't come too close." If you have an ultra-steep downward slope behind your house, which cannot be traversed easily, agave or yucca could be planted there to raise the energy. Do not ever plant thorny or spiky plants in the Relationship or Fortunate Blessings areas. You can make a Relationship area quite red and pink without the use of roses. I also do not recommend thorny or spiky plants near the entrance to your property, or near a pathway.

Not all spiky leaves can hurt you and not every plant with a spiky leaf form is forbidden. Most palm leaves are friendly and durable. Palms with floor uplights behind them enchant a ceiling of a room. If your ceiling is otherwise very plain in the dark hours, that splash of light and natural form can enhance the yang of the space. One particularly easy palm to grow is Rhapis Excelsa, the elegant Lady Palm. Palm experts refer to it as "the perfect indoor palm." Its use in the Fortunate Blessings area is on page 72.

Sansevieria (Snake Plant) has sword-shaped leaves, but they won't cut you. They require almost no light. But if given adequate sunlight, they will bear very fragrant white flowers. I would not place them indiscriminately in just any gua. Their use to change (uplift) energy around toilets is on page 85, and their use in the Fame area is on page 75.

CHAPTER 10

Retail Stores

The blunt truth about success in retail is this: You want a particular kind of chi energy people to:

- Come into your store
- Give you money
- Leave smiling

There is an old business adage, "The customer pays your salary." Your salary is a form of chi energy and it ultimately comes from the customer. You have exchanged the energy of your time for a paycheck. Remember what the customer is—a bundle of chi energy with money (another form of chi energy) in their pockets. This proper understanding of people as chi energy is the *most important* element for continued retail success.

THE FRONT

The first thing is to get your potential customer's attention. A good sign is often the first way to improve retail business by feng shui. Kat Wilson of *Back to the Drawing Board,* a sign company in San Francisco, says, "You only have a few seconds to get people's attention when they're on the street."

You get what you ask for with signage in retail. Very readable fat letters are a must. Fat letters say abundant and successful. Use fat, bountiful letters on door or street signs or any time the name of your business is presented to the public, such as on business cards and stationery.

If your business is located in a part of town that is multilingual, make sure some of your staff is multilingual and then *add it to your signage* and watch your business grow.

Carefully done, *neon is close to ultimate* for attracting chi energy during the dark hours. As far as the daylight hours are concerned, do not forget your number one goal. *Get their attention*—and do it well. One of the most important things is to use red on the outside. A red doormat is appropriate for many stores. If you are fortunate enough to have planters outside your door, grow red plants—leaf or flower color. Make maximum use of space in public view. In display windows and along the sidewalk use:

- Light
- Motion
- The color red

If you use the color green on an exterior sign, restrict it to less than one-fourth of the total size. Too much green will camouflage the sign.

PHYSICAL LAYOUT

One of the most important things not to do is to aim poison arrows at your customers as soon as they walk in the door by the right-angle edges of island display units and sales/wrap counters. I used to pass by a small charming bookstore that was doing just about everything wrong, feng shui-wise. I was quite fond of the store, and one day I offered the owner a bit of advice about the worst of the problems. The first island shelving unit was aiming a fierce poison arrow directly at the door. I had never seen a single customer in the store in all the times I had passed by it. I suggested that the owner move a spinning card rack in front of the offending corner. The next time I walked by the store, I saw that he had done so. I also saw that his small store had so many customers that I could not comfortably squeeze in the door. I walked on by, but with a big smile on my face.

Empower cashiers and any reception personnel by giving them a clear view of the door—without being in a direct line with the entrance. It is usually best not to have stairs in a direct line with the entrance door. If the stairs are not too close to the door, there is no problem.

Large stores often need support poles to hold up the roof. It is best to disguise them as much as possible. They can be incorporated into merchandise display.

The bagua in a retail store is exactly one hundred percent the same as the bagua in a residence. The same principles apply. (See page 70.) Read those pages and use this powerful feng shui tool for greater retail success. In particular, these five guas (in order of importance) should be enhanced:

- Fortunate Blessings
- Fame
- Relationship
- Helpful Friends
- Life's Path

The Fortunate Blessings gua is (as usual) of crucial importance. This area is a prime candidate for displaying your most expensive merchandise. Quite often, it is possible to enhance a gua by putting the correct color merchandise there. Do make sure that there is fairly direct access from the door to the Fortunate Blessings area. I have occasionally recommended that the entire back wall of a store be painted red (any shade). This can be helpful for bringing chi fully into a store and circulating it well. If you have ever considered having a fountain in your store, two of the best areas are near the cash register(s) and/or near the door. If your store has a sound system, I would not recommend playing the radio. The boosted volume of commercials is jarring to chi and rarely encourages customers to linger.

BUSINESS HOURS

Your store is like a fountain—it only works when it is on. A well-lighted open store attracts chi energy (including people).

Shopping at a store is a somewhat yang activity—compared to shopping on the Internet (the new competition). Internet sales can take place twenty-four hours a day. The least a store can do is to have an answering machine with its hours, preferably allowing the customer to leave a message. The time when your physical retail store is open to the public is vital time—the more the better. Working people work nine to five; after that, they are much more available to spend the money they've just earned. If you are not open evenings and weekends you are missing the boat. It's your best opportunity to "harvest" money, because these are the optimum shopping hours for many people. It is time-specific. Stores that have expanded their days and hours are often surprised by the effusion of gratitude coming from customers. That tells you everything.

CHAPTER 11

Offices

Many people are wary about where they work. They may have a feeling that something is wrong, but they can't quite put their finger on it, and even if they could, they might not feel empowered to do anything about it. Many owners and bosses discourage office changes or personalizing workspaces. They are shortsighted. A truly intelligent manager will allow (and encourage) workers to personalize their desks, as long as it isn't wildly out of place. The most important thing about your desk is that you be able to see the main door. If you cannot, use a mirror. If you have business cards, the Fame area of your desk is a very good place for them. As you are sitting at your desk, that area is in the far middle. A red business card holder would be an appropriate feng shui enhancement. Other tips for desks are in the sections on Empowered Positions (page 40) and Home Offices (page 105).

Because of computers and electronic technology, desks are often somewhat L-shaped. Where you spend most of your time at the desk determines the bagua—in most cases. Please be aware of the strong poison arrows that are often caused by these desk shapes and try not to sit in the path of one. (See Illustration #2, page 50.)

Your desk chair should be comfortable, and preferably have a solid back. Like a solid headboard, a desk chair that covers your back completely (without gaps) is considered ideal. It conveys the vibration of "solid backing" to your decisions. It can also serve to protect you from poison arrows coming from behind you.

Throughout the room or rooms of the office, apply the bagua map. Avoid having an open trash can in the Fortunate Blessings area. Instead, something striking like a large, healthy plant would be great.

WAITING ROOMS

Many professional offices (doctors, etc.) have waiting rooms. The most important factors to consider here include:

- Poison arrows. Do not let the shape of the reception desk cast a poison arrow at the entrance. Do not allow filing cabinets or other furniture to cast poison arrows at the reception personnel. Presumably no one client is going to be sitting in the waiting room for hours on end, day after day. Poison arrows (pointing at clients) are never a good idea, but you can certainly make do with them if you must. I would, however, refrain from using glass-top tables, unless the glass is rimmed.

- Appropriate empowerment. Empower the reception personnel by allowing a clear view of the entrance door. The reception desk should not be in a direct line with the entrance door. If there is no choice but to have a reception desk in a direct line with the entrance, then put a plant on the desk. Try to place it in a direct line between the door and the reception person. Always enhance these three areas: Fortunate Blessings, Fame, and Relationship. You won't be sorry! Depending on the type of office, also enhance the Health or Knowledge areas.

CHAPTER 12

Vehicles

When driving, it is essential to have your brain in gear. It would be preferable not to point a poison arrow right at your head with the sun visor. You can often get the same shading effect by pushing the visor outward toward the windshield. However, the most important thing in this case is visibility and safety.

Some of the guas that I recommend enhancing in a vehicle when traveling are:

- Travel/Helpful People

- Fortunate Blessings

- Relationship (if you have traveling companions)

Enhancing can mean a variety of things:

- Making sure those areas are clean and orderly

- This includes bumper stickers on the outside of a vehicle. If they are a faded or not relevant, remove them.

They really aren't directing fresh chi toward whatever cause they are espousing. The result is basically the opposite of what you had desired. Remove all traces of old bumper stickers, using the proper solvent if necessary.

Bumper stickers are not objectionable if:

- They are removed when old or faded.

- Consideration is given to what the sticker is saying in relation to the gua in which it is placed.

- There are not too many. Too many are all talking at once and therefore have lost most of their impact. Feng shui doesn't care whether or not you have bumper stickers, but too many is definitely a no-no.

People have different needs when it comes to hanging things from rearview mirrors or ornamenting dashboards. Many teachers recommend hanging a small, reflective silver ball from your rearview mirror. These are called mayan balls. A small crystal will enhance any area. Do more if you are inclined to do so, but do absolutely nothing that would impede the visibility and safety.

CARS

A basic feng shui rule is that the more time you spend in a particular place, the more you are affected by that place. The more you are in a particular car, the more it affects you. An object that changes direction as frequently as a car does not lend itself to compass-oriented feng shui. Entrance-based bagua is the only method to use on most cars. The mouth of chi (or entrance) is where you open the hood to access the motor. So, if you open the front hood to get to the motor, your Fortunate Blessings area includes the back left bumper, some of the interior of the trunk, and some of the left back seat area. Cars with no back seat often have none of the Fortunate Blessings area in the "people part" of the car.

If the engine is in the back of the car, then the mouth of chi is in the back of the car and the bagua orientation flips around. In this case, the Fame area is where the hood ornament is, or would be.

TRUCKS, VANS, AND RVS

The model of the engine as the "mouth of chi" for cars holds true for most other types of vehicles. There is, however, another orientation of the bagua.

In a camper or vehicle that you sleep in, there is an additional bagua based on the door that is used to access the living area. If the living area is not accessible from the driver's area, the most influential bagua for that living area is based on its "people door." The bed of a pickup truck has a bagua that is based on the tailgate as entrance. If there is a camper shell over the bed of the truck, that particular bagua has significantly more impact because it is an enclosed space.

Recommended Books

As someone begins to read about feng shui, first they are intrigued. Then, as they read more, they get confused. The confusion inevitably comes from the fact that one of feng shui's most powerful tools, a grid called the bagua, is used very differently by two different (and equally popular) schools of feng shui, compass oriented and entrance oriented. The problem is further compounded by the fact that almost never does a single book mention that there is another way to do it. It's not much of a problem when feng shui schools disagree about fairly minor things, like mirrors in a bedroom. But placement of the bagua is major in feng shui. Most other aspects of feng shui are either universal or their differences are differences of emphasis. I have divided my recommendations into those books that use the entrance to orient the bagua and those which use the compass. Last I list books on topics that are related to feng shui. For more book reviews, please consult my website, www.fungshway.com, which is devoted to reviewing feng shui literature.

COMPASS ORIENTATION

The Chinese year and the Western year don't coincide exactly. When reading any charts where you are required to look up a certain year, be aware that the Chinese year can begin as late as February 20. The Chinese timing of the beginning of each new year is based on the moon. It is not less exact than the Western (Gregorian) calendar, it simply deals with of leap years more naturally. If the chart gives only the Western year (i.e., 1976) with no months mentioned and if you were born in January (or the first weeks in February), you may need to read the previous year (i.e., 1975). If the Compass School book you are using does not mention specific days, consult Appendix III, Chinese Astrological Signs and Elements, on page 187.

COMPLETE ILLUSTRATED GUIDE TO FENG SHUI BY LILLIAN TOO

224 pages. Element Books, Rockport, Maine, 1996.
This is a magnum opus of compass-based feng shui. It is a very thorough book and extremely well illustrated. It might be overwhelming for a beginner, but it's clearly written and could end up being the only compass-school feng shui book you would need. Too's books are always recognizable by the unique illustrations (cut paper) and they do get the point across.

Personal Feng Shui Manual: How to Develop a Healthy and Harmonious Lifestyle by Kam Chuen Lam

159 pages. Henry Holt and Company, New York, 1998. This book is a joy to read or open at any time. The phenomenally good watercolor illustrations deliver the message. If you've ever wondered how chi energy moves, you'll know after you've looked at this book. The birth date charts are laid out in an user-friendly way. In some other books, when the charts are handled badly, it only serves to frustrate beginners.

Simple Feng Shui by Damian Sharp

112 pages. Conari Press, Berkeley, California, 1999. I recommend having this book with you if you're shopping to buy a house. It has the clearest information on the external environment. There's an especially good section on how the element of your house (or lot) interacts with the larger landscape of your area. Many books have tried to present this very complicated information in an understandable way. But trying and succeeding are very different things. Sharp has succeeded with a rare lucidity, so much so that what seemed complicated before will seem simple now. When he explains the Taoist teaching of the five elements, he doesn't belabor trying to teach you Taoism. He just gets right to how it affects your environment. The basic chi that first comes into our lives does so under the influence of the larger environment. Do not underestimate its importance!

ENTRANCE ORIENTATION

FENG SHUI FOR YOUR HOME
BY SARAH SHURETY

140 pages. Rider Publishing, London, 1997.

This book is extremely well written, and the pictures and layout make the information quite understandable. Shurety is one of the very few authors who include a chapter on Directionology (finding out which direction is good to move toward in any given year). Like all her chapters, it is well explained and easy to use. The venerable publisher, Rider, is England's premier metaphysical publisher, and they do know how to do a book right. It is well edited and it truly does its subject justice. The section on color is not overly long, but it is power-packed. Her section on shapes of headboards is very illuminating and, once again, not a common feature of most books.

FENG SHUI: HARMONY BY DESIGN
BY NANCY SANTO PIETRO

219 pages. Berkley Publishing, New York, 1996. This book is a brilliant achievement, dealing primarily with the interior of a house. It has some of the most lucid prose and drawings to be found in any feng shui book. It even includes advice on how to get pregnant! It also contains information on aromatherapy, crystal and gemstone properties, and the chakras. This book stands head and shoulders above most others.

FENG SHUI HOUSE BOOK
BY GINA LAZENBY

160 pages. Watson Guptill, New York, 1998.

I recommend this book wholeheartedly — it is glorious. The pictures are accompanied by extensive commentary. She does what almost no other author does — she comments on *everything* in the picture and goes the extra mile by pointing out what else could be done to improve it. She can say in one sentence what other authors require a paragraph for.

TAOIST FENG SHUI
BY SUSAN LEVITT

148 pages. Destiny Books (Inner Traditions), Rochester, Vermont 2000.

Feng shui is a Taoist art, intertwined with the *I Ching* and Chinese astrology. Levitt's chapter on astrology, called "Reckoning of Fate," is the best of its kind in any book I've seen. The illustration on page 10 shows how the eight trigrams come from the basic straight yin and yang. The book even delivers a full *I Ching*. Quite empowering.

The illustrations are well conceived and executed. You *will* know how to practice feng shui once you've read this book, and you will also have a deeper understanding of its Taoist roots. This book is for everyone. Her writing is very clear and it has my highest recommendation.

Wind and Water : Your Personal Feng Shui Journey
by Carol Hyder

257 pages. The Crossing Press, Freedom, California, (800)777-1048, www.crossingpress.com, 1998.

This book has much to recommend it. Its convenient size makes it a "carry around with you" kind of book. You almost feel as though you are reading aphorisms or daily reminders. No section is more than one page long and they are chock full of information. Hyder makes the reader understand more deeply what feng shui changes are all about. She gives you an introspective knowledge of feng shui. Here are some of her chapter headings: "Points of Focus," "Inner Strength," "Clarity," "Honoring Yourself," and "Inner Wisdom."

Wind and Water Audio Version also available from The Crossing Press. 160 minutes-4 cassette tapes.

Feng Shui Journal
Quarterly Magazine

About 45 pages. Published by Feng Shui Warehouse, San Diego, California (800) 399-1599, website fengshuiwh.com. An ecumenical magazine representing many schools of feng shui and related topics. The articles have a get-down-to-business feel. It can be hard to find on newsstands.

RELATED TOPICS

THE BOOK OF CHANGES
AND THE UNCHANGING TRUTH
BY NI, HUA CHING

732 pages. SevenStar Communications, (800) 578-9526, www.taostar.com, 1993.

The *I Ching* is considered by many to be the oldest written book in the world. It is a Taoist oracle—a wise friend offering advice in troublesome situations. It is not advisable to overuse it. It offers a *larger* view, often giving very specific lucid advice in situations that really have you stumped.

Whether or not one connects well with this fine book largely depends upon the translation that you use. There are now many *I Ching* translations. The Wilhelm/Baynes translation from Princeton University Press is the old standard, but I feel that *The Book of Changes and the Unchanging Truth* is now the finest translation available. Master Ni is from an ancient lineage of Taoist masters. He knows with his bones what he is translating. I unreservedly recommend this translation.

Getting Organized
by Stephanie Winston

Audiotape, 54 minutes. Simon & Schuster, 1986.

Organizing is basic to feng shui, but sayin' it and doin' it are two very different things! For some people, to be organized is a major lifestyle challenge. The outcome can seem attractive, but getting from here to there can be daunting. The good news is that this audio tape of *Getting Organized* can seep into you like osmosis. Keep listening to it until you are doing it—all of it. Stephanie Winston does cover all of it, every aspect of being organized. Her voice carries a confidence that helps get you there. I've read scores of organizing books, and this one stands high—especially the tape version.

Speed Cleaning
by Jeff Campbell

The Clean Team, www.thecleanteam.com, 800-717-2532. 119 pages. Dell, New York, 1987.

Cleaning is as essential to feng shui as breathing is to life. This is by far the best book on cleaning ever published. It should be taught in schools, because sooner or later everybody's gotta do some cleaning—may as well be smart about it. As in feng shui, this book isn't afraid to state the obvious. Some rules are shockingly simple, as in, "work from top to bottom," "if it isn't dirty, don't clean it," "pay attention," but when applied together, they make for fast, efficient cleaning.

Spring Cleaning
by Jeff Campbell

191 pages. Dell, New York, 1989. Jeff Campbell's *Speed Cleaning* covers the weekly or (biweekly) basics and this subsequent book covers just about all the rest. Just about everybody has windows, and way too many are dirty most of the time. It is empowering to have the knowledge and skill to clean one's windows quickly and efficiently. He gives step-by-step instructions for every conceivable kind of window. No paper towels, no newspapers, no blue chemical spray, and no streaks! A good squeegee is your friend.

Campbell gives you the do's and don'ts of polishing metal, how to clean carpets, floors, and walls, and much more. I rarely have need to do some of the things this book covers (i.e., strip a floor), but should the need arise, I know I can count on Jeff Campbell to have done *all* the research for me. Even though he explains in detail how to wash a ceiling, his first advice is don't (unless you absolutely have to). He is reasonable, readable, and wonderful. I recommend this book unreservedly. Every homeowner and probably every renter should have a copy of this fine book.

Glossary

Bagua mirror

Typically this kind of mirror is rather small. The frame has eight sides with *I Ching* trigrams around the outside and a round mirror in the center. The background is red and the trigrams are gold. It is primarily for exterior use. See Approach, page 13.

Casement window

To open these windows, a crank handle is turned, and the windows open out on hinges along the vertical edge. If there is a screen, it is on the inside of the glass. Frank Lloyd Wright said that if these windows had not already been invented, he would have invented them. They are treasured for their ability to "catch a breeze" and funnel it into a room. Feng shui loves them because they can (usually) open fully.

Chi
Energy. The basic stuff of all life and existence. See page 27.

Compass school
This is the second oldest school of feng shui. The oldest school (Landform) is from the mountains of China. Much of its teachings apply only to "interesting" terrain. Compass feng shui originated on the flat plains of China. Rugged mountains affect the microclimate and the chi of an area. In a flat featureless terrain, it is the directions that exert the most apparent environmental influence.

Concave
A mirror surface that goes inward (like a "cave"). See Mirrors, page 120.

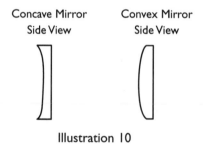

Concave Mirror Side View · Convex Mirror Side View

Illustration 10

Convex
A mirror surface that bulges outward. See Mirrors, page 120, and The Exterior, page 13.

Directionology

Taoist astrology and numerology can tell you which directions are best (and worst) for you to move towards. The calculations are based upon when you were born. Each year the auspicious directions will change. You are considered to be in the center of the compass.

Double-Hung window

These windows were popular in your great-grandparents' time and they are still much used today. The bottom half slides up and (hopefully) the top slides down. They are not a feng shui favorite because the window opening is always at least half blocked by the glass. In my experience, many double-hung windows become painted shut over time. Unstick 'em, for God's sake! Actually, you'll be doing it for your own sake. They were meant to function fully and they've been made dysfunctional by some layers of paint. Hardware and paint stores sell a special tool for doing the job. It is shaped like a flat trowel with serrated edges. Be sure to use a mask so that you don't breathe (potentially lead-contaminated) paint dust. Once both halves of the window can open well, you'll have restored better air circulation to the building and eliminated some disfunction from your life. Even so, double-hung windows are never as ideal as windows that can open fully.

Elements

There are five elements according to Taoism. The word *element* here has absolutely nothing to do with the Periodic Table of Elements of Western science. *In Taoism they refer to archetypal energies.* The elements are:

- Water

- Wood

- Fire

- Metal

- Earth

See the chart of Bagua Areas on pages 60 and 61.

Fame area

One of the nine areas in the bagua map. It is concerned with what is being said about you. See Individual Bagua Areas, page 72.

Fortunate Blessings area

One of the nine areas in the bagua map. It is typically called the Wealth area and, as such, has become a buzzword for feng shui. See Individual Bagua Areas, page 72.

Gua or Guas

The Chinese name for any of the nine bagua areas. Guas is the plural. See page 57.

Magnetic sleep pad

A pad with magnets in it, which usually goes under your mattress, providing an even, negative, magnetic field for your body. There are several reputable manufacturers. One is MAGNETICo, in Calgary, Alberta, Canada 800-265-1119, www.magneticosleep.com.

Poison arrow

This (malevolent) chi energy has various names: *sha chi*, or *shar*. It is chi energy that has encountered something in the environment to cause it to speed up, get irritated, or become stagnant. See Poison Arrows, page 47.

Risers

Risers are the vertical parts of stairs that connect the treads, which you step on. When you walk upstairs they are the part that your toes are pointing towards. See page 33.

Trigram

The basic unit of a trigram is a line, either solid or with an opening in it.

━━ ━━   ━━━━━

A yin line with   A solid yang
an opening   line
in the center

When combined in units of three lines, there are only eight possible combinations. They are listed with their meanings in the chart of Bagua Areas on pages 60 and 61. Also see Recommended Books, *The Book of Changes and the Unchanging Truth*—an excellent translation of the *I Ching* which explains trigrams.

Chinese Astrological Signs and Elements

Year	Sign	Element	Western Dates
1910	Dog	Metal	10 Feb 1910–29 Jan 1911
1911	Pig	Metal	30 Jan 1911–17 Feb 1912
1912	Rat	Water	18 Feb 1912–5 Feb 1913
1913	Ox	Water	6 Feb 1913–25 Jan 1914
1914	Tiger	Wood	26 Jan 1914–13 Feb 1915
1915	Hare	Wood	14 Feb 1915–2 Feb 1916
1916	Dragon	Fire	3 Feb 1916–22 Jan 1917
1917	Snake	Fire	23 Jan 1917–10 Feb 1918
1918	Horse	Earth	11 Feb 1918–31 Jan 1919
1919	Sheep	Earth	1 Feb 1919–19 Feb 1920
1920	Monkey	Metal	20 Feb 1920–7 Feb 1921
1921	Rooster	Metal	8 Feb 1921–27 Jan 1922
1922	Dog	Water	28 Jan 1922–15 Feb 1923

Year	Sign	Element	Western Dates
1923	Pig	Water	16 Feb 1923–4 Feb 1924
1924	Rat	Wood	5 Feb 1924–24 Jan 1925
1925	Ox	Wood	25 Jan 1925–12 Feb 1926
1926	Tiger	Fire	13 Feb 1926–1 Feb 1927
1927	Hare	Fire	2 Feb 1927–22 Jan 1928
1928	Dragon	Earth	23 Jan 1928–9 Feb 1929
1929	Snake	Earth	10 Feb 1929–29 Jan 1930
1930	Horse	Metal	30 Jan 1930–16 Feb 1931
1931	Sheep	Metal	17 Feb 1931–5 Feb 1932
1932	Monkey	Water	6 Feb 1932–25 Jan 1933
1933	Rooster	Water	26 Jan 1933–13 Feb 1934
1934	Dog	Wood	14 Feb 1934–3 Feb 1935
1935	Pig	Wood	4 Feb 1935–23 Jan 1936
1936	Rat	Fire	24 Jan 1936–10 Feb 1937
1937	Ox	Fire	11 Feb 1937–30 Jan 1938
1938	Tiger	Earth	31 Jan 1938–18 Feb 1939
1939	Hare	Earth	19 Feb 1939–7 Feb 1940
1940	Dragon	Metal	8 Feb 1940–26 Jan 1941
1941	Snake	Metal	27 Jan 1941–14 Feb 1942
1942	Horse	Water	15 Feb 1942–4 Feb 1943
1943	Sheep	Water	5 Feb 1943–24 Jan 1944

Year	Sign	Element	Western Dates
1944	Monkey	Wood	25 Jan 1944–12 Feb 1945
1945	Rooster	Wood	13 Feb 1945–1 Feb 1946
1946	Dog	Fire	2 Feb 1946–21 Jan 1947
1947	Pig	Fire	22 Jan 1947–9 Feb 1948
1948	Rat	Earth	10 Feb 1948–28 Jan 1949
1949	Ox	Earth	29 Jan 1949–16 Feb 1950
1950	Tiger	Metal	17 Feb 1950–5 Feb 1951
1951	Hare	Metal	6 Feb 1951–26 Jan 1952
1952	Dragon	Water	27 Jan 1952–13 Feb 1953
1953	Snake	Water	14 Feb 1953–2 Feb 1954
1954	Horse	Wood	3 Feb 1954–23 Jan 1955
1955	Sheep	Wood	24 Jan 1955–11 Feb 1956
1956	Monkey	Fire	12 Feb 1956–30 Jan 1957
1957	Rooster	Fire	31 Jan 1957–17 Feb 1958
1958	Dog	Earth	18 Feb 1958–7 Feb 1959
1959	Pig	Earth	8 Feb 1959–27 Jan 1960
1960	Rat	Metal	28 Jan 1960–14 Feb 1961
1961	Ox	Metal	15 Feb 1961–4 Feb 1962
1962	Tiger	Water	5 Feb 1962–24 Jan 1963
1963	Hare	Water	25 Jan 1963–12 Feb 1964
1964	Dragon	Wood	13 Feb 1964–1 Feb 1965

Year	Sign	Element	Western Dates
1965	Snake	Wood	2 Feb 1965–20 Jan 1966
1966	Horse	Fire	21 Jan 1966–8 Feb 1967
1967	Sheep	Fire	9 Feb 1967–29 Jan 1968
1968	Monkey	Earth	30 Jan 1968–16 Feb 1969
1969	Rooster	Earth	17 Feb 1969–5 Feb 1970
1970	Dog	Metal	6 Feb 1970–26 Jan 1971
1971	Pig	Metal	27 Jan 1971–14 Feb 1972
1972	Rat	Water	15 Feb 1972–2 Feb 1973
1973	Ox	Water	3 Feb 1973–22 Jan 1974
1974	Tiger	Wood	23 Jan 1974–10 Feb 1975
1975	Hare	Wood	11 Feb 1975–30 Jan 1976

BOOKS BY THE CROSSING PRESS

Fundamentals of Hawaiian Mysticism

By Charlotte Berney

Evolving in isolation on an island paradise, the mystical practice of Huna has shaped the profound yet elegantly simple Hawaiian character. Charlotte Berney presents Huna traditions as they apply to words, prayer, gods, the breath, a loving spirit, family ties, nature, and mana.

$12.95 • Paper • ISBN 1-58091-026-2

Fundamentals of Jewish Mysticm and Kabbalah

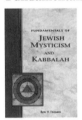

By Ron Feldman

This concise introductory book explains what Kabbalah is and how study of its text and practices enhance the life of the soul and the holiness of the body.

$12.95 • Paper • ISBN 1-58091-049-1

Fundamentals of Tibetan Buddhism

By Rebecca McClen Novick

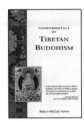

This book explores the history, philosophy, and practice of Tibetan Buddhism. Novick's concise history of Buddhism, and her explanations of the Four Noble Truths, Wheel of Life, Karma, Five Paths, Six Perfections, and the different schools of thought within the Buddhist teachings help us understand Tibetan Buddhism as a way of experiencing the world, more than as a religion or philosophy.

$12.95 • Paper • ISBN 0-89594-953-9

A Little Book of Love Magic

By Patricia Telesco

A cornucopia of lore, magic, and imaginative ritual designed to bring excitement and romance to your life. Patricia Telesco tells us how to use magic to manifest our hopes and dreams for romantic relationships, friendships, family relations, and passions for our work.

$9.95 • Paper • ISBN 0-89594-887-7